How to Win an Election

Paul Richards is an author, broadcaster and campaigner.

He has been a Labour parliamentary candidate twice – at Billericay at the 1997 General Election and at Lewes at the 2001 General Election. He has served on Labour's campaign teams for over a dozen by-elections all over the UK, as well as during local, national and European elections. He was a local government candidate in 1994 and 1998.

As director of Paul Richards Communications Limited, he provides advice to a variety of organisations in the public, private and voluntary sectors.

His first book, published in 1998, was *Be Your Own Spin Doctor – A practical guide to using the media,* which has stayed in the Politico's best-seller list for over two years.

Paul has written various political pamphlets, including *Long to Reign Over Us?* (a study into the future of the monarchy), *Is the Party Over? New Labour and the Politics of Participation, The Case for Socialism* (with an introduction by Tony Blair) and the Labour candidates' guide, *Using the Media*.

He often appears on radio and television, including *Wogan, Today, Newsnight, The Moral Maze* and a variety of other programmes.

Paul Richards is married to Sarah, and they live in Southfields in southwest London.

How to Win an Election

The Art of Political Campaigning

Paul Richards

First published in Great Britain 2001
by Politico's Publishing
8 Artillery Row, London, SW1P 1RZ, England

Tel. 020 7931 0090
Email publishing@politicos.co.uk
Website http://www.politicos.co.uk/publishing

Printed and bound in Great Britain by Creative Design and Print.
Typeset in Legacy by Duncan Brack.

ILLUSTRATIONS
The photographs on pages 5
Liberal Democrat News.

Contents

Foreword *by* Paul Routledge

It is a head-shaking business. Why do so many men and women want to run the country? Why do they want to tell other people how to lead their lives, when so many of them are manifestly incapable of running their own?

The answer to this mystery has eluded serious and flippant observers alike. When asked straight out, Labour politicians mumble something about social justice and making the world a better place. Tony Blair is very good at this mock-modest dishonesty. Occasionally, a splenetic Tory will spit out 'To stop the likes of you taking over!', which at least has the virtue of being true.

Motive is an engaging theme, particularly at by-elections when the candidates may legitimately be subjected to withering scrutiny in pursuit of something entertaining to put in the newspaper. I remember Matthew Taylor, the Liberal Democrat contender at Truro, giving a brilliant performance of his prepared spiel. And very pleased with himself he was, too. I chewed my biro and offered that he sounded too good to be true. 'I'm not too good to be true!' he hollered, adding for good measure that he wanted to become the Norman Tebbit of his party. Another intro in the can.

Perhaps he should have heeded the advice of former Tory party treasurer Alistair McAlpine to his nephew: 'You wish to enter politics? I strongly advise you against it, for in the public's eye it is a profession worse regarded than breaking and entering. You will become fair game for the press, and for any creature who chooses to blackmail you. You will become the butt of humour on television. Vile accusations will be made to you across the dinner table, and worse still, when people listen with reverence to what you tell them, then you will know in your heart that you are failing.'

Of course, these days wannabe politicians are not born or fashioned by hard circumstances. They are produced, certainly by the two main parties, in a mysterious *X Files* factory on a trading estate somewhere in middle England. They are programmed by twenty-somethings who have been to the USA and 'worked with the winner's campaign team', which means they were suffered to follow them round for a few days. They have read about focus groups, and they imagine Philip Gould is a guru, not a wordy fool.

Naturally, they need a bible on their trek to Westminster, and Paul Richards has provided it with *How to Win an Election*. His manual, essentially aimed at Parliamentary hopefuls, will admirably fill in the gaps left by Millbank's brain-implant team. But it also exposes the terrifying political hollowness at the heart of the Blairite project. This is a book about getting in, and to hell with purpose.

Occasionally, reading down the list of a Commons division, I exclaim: 'Some of these names are made up! They are not real people. I have never seen them at Westminster, or heard them speak.' They must have read an early draft of this manual, which tells them how to bamboozle the electorate, but not why. Few would echo Martin Bell's desire for 'principled politics', while agreeing with his wish to do something breathtakingly foolhardy, just once in a while. Yet he won, against the formidable Tory Party machine.

Because, fortunately, winning elections is an inexact science. Simply being chosen is something of a lottery. Roy Hattersley allegedly tried thirty-two constituencies before he found one that wanted him. Yvette Cooper, the Commons pin-up most likely to be Labour's first woman leader, almost gave up hope until she landed Pontefract & Castleford in the teeth of male chauvinist opposition. John Bercow, the mouthy Tory new boy, helicoptered from one adoption meeting to another to win his nomination. Even Betty Boothroyd had five goes before getting to Westminster. Which just goes to show that determination is worth a thousand recommendations from the Fire Brigades Union, though it was the firemen who gave Sedgefield to Tony Blair.

How to Win an Election comes, contrarily, at the end of a well-trodden path, after Gerald Kaufman's *How to be a Minister* and Paul Flynn's *Commons Knowledge: How to be a Backbencher*. Kaufman's entertaining minor classic is based on experience, and Flynn's tongue-in-cheek offering reflects the frustrations of life on the back-benches. Alas for the author of a 'how to' manual, Richards has not actually made the prescription work to his own advantage. Fifteen years of devoted service to Labour has so far failed to get him a winnable seat in local government or Westminster.

Perhaps he should take to heart the old story told in Glasgow by a veteran Labour hard-hat. Enthusiastic young candidate to party organiser : 'But I don't think I can win this seat.' He replied: 'Dinna worry, son. If we thought we had a hope in hell of winning this seat, you wouldnae be the candidate!'

Paul Routledge
The Mirror, *February 2001*

Acknowledgments

Thanks to Luke Akehurst, John Arnold, Tony Brown, Iain Dale and all at Politico's, Mark Glover, Ruth Turner, all those who preferred to remain anonymous, and most of all to Sarah Richards for her continuing support and excellent advice. Thanks are due to the members of the Lewes Labour Party, and everyone with whom I've campaigned over the past fifteen years.

Any mistakes are the author's alone.

Paul Richards
February 2001

Preface

Is Politics an Art or a Science?

If only it were that simple. If only someone with some experience of election campaigns could sit down and write a book entitled *How to Win an Election* and reveal some set of rules and procedures which made electoral victory inevitable. If only electorates were so utterly open to manipulation and persuasion that politicians could pull levers and press buttons, say the right things and stand on the right platforms, and votes would fall like leaves from the trees.

The reality is that elections are never that simple. They defy attempts at categorisation and definition. No one election campaign is exactly the same as another. Campaigns have their own life, their own defining moments, their own personality. Individuals' memories of them vary, like soldiers on the battlefield, depending on their role, and which side they fought on. What works well in one campaign can be a disaster in the next. Political parties are often like the British Army – always prepared to fight the last war, not the next. John Major's soapbox added to his unpretentious 'normal bloke' appeal in the 1992 general election and, along with not being Margaret Thatcher, helped him to victory over Labour. By the 1997 general election, the soapbox was seen as a metaphor for the out-of-date and ramshackle state of his party, and he lost.

Issues which dominate in one election can be irrelevant the next. Elections are fought against the backdrop of specific historical moments, and owe their ebb and flow to the social and economic forces at work at any one time. Edward Heath went to the country against a backdrop of a miners' strike and rocketing oil prices; his question to the voters was 'who governs Britain?' ('Not you', came the reply).

Wars create their own electoral circumstances. In 1900, Salisbury's Conservatives won the 'khaki election' on a wave of patriotic fervour during the Boer War. Lloyd George won another 'khaki election' in 1918 by promising the returning soldiers and their families a land fit for heroes. In 1945, the war led to a Labour landslide. In 1983, after trailing in the polls, Margaret Thatcher won a massive victory, helped by her success in the Falklands War.

No election is fought in isolation from events. In 1992, tax dominated the agenda, but not so much in 1997. Issues become salient which few could have predicted. In September 2000, Britain nearly ground to a halt because of protests over petrol prices – yet no politician, and certainly not the Government, had anticipated it or was prepared.

Candidates who are seen as rising stars can turn quickly to has-beens or never-weres. History is littered with the failed careers of politicians who were named as future Prime Ministers. Remember Bryan Gould or John Moore? Exactly.

Elections are never predictable. Who would have thought that Winston Churchill, who had led Britain through its greatest test in 1940, would be heavily defeated in the general election of 1945? In 1997, Tony Blair won a massive victory against a discredited Conservative Government. Surely Labour could not lose the 2001 general election? Surely the British public wouldn't want William Hague as Prime Minister instead of Tony Blair? History has taught us not to be so sure.

Even those closest to the action cannot discern what fate is about to deliver. In April 1970, Prime Minister Harold Wilson, always fond of a football metaphor, said '*If I were a football manager, on present form I would be more worried about job security than I am as Prime Minister.*' In June 1970, Wilson lost the general election. His confidence was not born of the bravado that all politicians display ahead of an election. No politician ever concedes the possibility of defeat, no matter how likely. No, Wilson's confidence was based on all the signs of victory being in place. He was the incumbent Prime Minister. His opinion poll ratings were good. He had a sound majority in the House of Commons. Journalists, commentators, even the politicians themselves, were all convinced that Labour was set for a third election victory. On polling day, Nora Beloff, the *Observer's* political correspondent had written her article on why Labour had won, and knocked off early. The *Sunday Times* wrote 'Mr Wilson is heading straight back to Downing Street', *The Times* stated 'it is too late for the Conservatives to recover lost ground' and the *Evening Standard* said 'Labour will certainly win'.

But the voters had other ideas.

You don't need a Master's in political theory to understand why there is this randomness and unpredictability to elections. It is because elections are about people, and people are entirely beyond scientific calculation, interpretation, or prediction. People are unpredictable. Often we behave in irrational and unexpected ways. That goes for our behaviour in elections as much as choosing a brand of washing-up liquid. Modern political parties and media companies employ armies of pollsters, behavioural scientists, sociologists, psephologists and strategists – the modern mercenaries of politics – to devise new and better ways to mine the popular psyche and prospect for votes. They study past election results, look at voting behaviour across age, sex, race and place, conduct focus groups into what motivates people, test out new slogans, policies, even colours, and try to devise what will get you to the polling station and put your cross in the right box. The political scientist Angelo Panebianco claims that modern political parties are now run by these guns-for-hire, moving from campaign to campaign, selling their skills to the highest bidder. He claims the modern party has become an 'electoral-professional party'.

But despite all the science employed to win your support, the only thing a study of politics tells us is that politics is an art. The unlikeliest politicians prosper, the least likely campaign strategies succeed, and history is made through unpredictable events. How else do you explain the victory of George W. Bush? In a democracy where there is a choice of parties and candidates, voters will make their minds up for themselves. Politicians may try to press all the right buttons, but can never, with confidence, take any vote for granted. An election campaign which consumes millions of pounds of resources – posters, advertising, television broadcasts, and direct mail – can be scuppered by the voter in the polling booth who votes for the candidate who has the same name as their husband, or the same colour as their football team, or against the politician who didn't answer their letter. In those brief moments in a polling station, on a wet Thursday, in one of a thousand towns and villages, the skills of Disraeli and Churchill and Lloyd George, the writings of Plato and Rousseau and Marx, the efforts of the great political parties, and the dreams of a thousand expectant candidates are reduced to a snap decision and a cross drawn with a stubby pencil.

So winning elections is not a simple business. There are no iron laws of politics, just trends and fads, which as soon as the politicians have caught up with, the people have moved on. Like an ageing swinger trying to keep up with his teenage sons and daughters, no sooner has one political fashion been mastered than another one comes along to replace it.

Election campaigns themselves are buffeted by unforeseen circumstances and the actions of your electoral opponents. No campaign runs according to plan. Scandals break across the neatly plotted campaign grids; issues blow the media schedules off course. Labour's 1992 campaign plan, planned for years, was destroyed in minutes by a saga known as Jennifer's Ear. In 1997, the Conservatives' desire to get their positive message across was squashed by the unfolding drama in Tatton, where Martin Bell, the man in the white suit, took on Neil Hamilton. Campaigns are dominated by what Harold Macmillan called 'events, dear boy, events'. Campaigns are fluid, not static, and as in war, success comes from adaptability and innovation as much as from sticking to an agreed set of tactics.

So, as the Soviet Foreign Minister Molotov once said to Ernest Bevin, 'the disadvantage of free elections is that you can never be sure who is going to win them.' This reality is, of course, entirely welcome. The vagaries and irrationalities of democratic systems should be cherished and defended, not decried. When the results of elections have been predictable in the past, usually the only reason is because one set of politicians has had the other set of politicians banned, imprisoned or shot. You can have any party as long as it's us.

So if elections are unpredictable, and voters will always defy the pollsters' and pundits' rune-reading and sooth-saying, how can politicians ever hope to construct their policy platforms and conduct their campaigns? Is there any point to a book called *How to Win an Election*. Have you been cheated of the cover price?

Well, no.

Politics is an art. As the American politician Mario Cuomo puts it 'you campaign in poetry.' (The second part of Cuomo's aphorism is that 'you govern in prose' but that's another story.) Successful politicians have an energy, a flair, a quality which inspires trust and loyalty. Others win because they aren't as bad as the other bloke. There are plenty of intelligent, skilled men and women in politics who practice the art with aplomb.

Some are born campaigners, who like nothing better than knocking on doors, meeting the voters, and soapbox oratory. Like Roy Hattersley, many get the bug early, as he recalls from the 1950 election: 'it had been love at first sight ... with the irresistible canvass-cards and the marked-up registers that could not be denied.' For them, politics is all about meeting the voters and engaging in the doorstep debates.

But there's more to it than a cheery candidate, a stack of leaflets and some stout shoes. As well as the artistry of the campaign, there is science too. There are components and building-blocks of a campaign which are crucial to standing a chance. There are the techniques tested against real experience and real elections, and the accumulated knowledge of a thousand campaigns and campaigners. There are plenty of representative politicians in office today all over the world who owe their positions of power not to having better ideas or even a majority of support, but thanks to better organisation. The result of the 2000 US Presidential election, decided on the tiniest of margins, was won on organisation – the ability to get out the vote.

The lessons from recent elections, and some of the timeless axioms of political campaigning are what this book is all about. Just as the Greeks and Romans taught their elite young men *rhetoric*, the art of public debate and argument, so the modern aspirant politician can learn the art of campaigning. Mostly, what follows is about political elections at a local or national level. But there are plenty of tricks and tips which are as valid for an election to become president of the golf club as a Member of Parliament.

Throughout the book I refer to 'you'. The 'you' I am addressing is the person most likely to be reading a book called *How to Win an Election*, namely someone who is standing, or considering standing, for office. I hope that the advice herein is of direct benefit to candidates standing for whatever office, high or low. But the reader interested in politics will find plenty to amuse them as well. Politics can be a fun spectator sport as well as one to play.

For most of its players, politics is an obsession. The actual work of an election campaign, especially at the local level, is hard, dull and thankless. By definition, because there are always more candidates than elected positions available, the bulk of the effort of an election results in your candidate losing. In 1997, 3724 candidates stood for Parliament, an average of

5.6 per constituency, and 3065 of them lost. Election campaigns are not for the faint-hearted or those with a low boredom threshold. Canvassing householders may seem fun at first, but after weeks of it you never want to see another doorbell, letter-box or Staffordshire bull terrier again.

The playwright David Hare wrote a play after observing the 1992 general election, called *The Absence of War*. The quote, which came from campaign guru Philip Gould, implies that in peacetime the combative energies of political leaders are devoted to election campaigns. In the play the character Andrew Buchan says: 'I have a theory. People of my age, we did not fight in a war. If you fight in a war, you have some sense of personal worth. So now we seek it by keeping busy. We work, and we hope we will do good.'

Indeed much of the lexicon of political campaigning is redolent, or even directly taken, from military terminology: 'war room', 'war book', 'war chest', 'rank and file', 'battleground seats', 'opening salvos', 'big guns', even 'campaign' itself.

I totted up the number of elections I have stood in over the past fifteen years, and including the election to the Secretary of my school Sixth Form committee which was rigged in my favour by a friend, postal ballots for the executives of various political bodies, uncontested elections for positions no-one else was foolish enough to want, and standing unsuccessfully for the council twice and Parliament once, the total is more than thirty. As I write, I am Labour's prospective parliamentary candidate in Lewes, East Sussex, a seat Labour has never won. In the 1997 general election I took on Euro-sceptic Teresa Gorman in Billericay. This time I am against the maverick Liberal Norman Baker. As well as standing as a candidate myself, I have helped various good people in their elections. Since becoming involved in politics, I have helped campaign in more than a dozen by-elections including Liverpool Walton in 1990, Newbury, Christchurch, Dudley West, Tamworth, Littleborough and Saddleworth, Uxbridge, Beckenham, Eddisbury, Kensington and Chelsea and, in November 2000, Preston. At each of these by-elections I have knocked on doors, canvassed voters, attended rallies and meetings, and helped get out the vote on polling day. I have been rained on in Beckenham and caught sunburn in Chelsea. I have been chased by Militant supporters in Liverpool, and picketed by the National Front in Uxbridge. And in each one I have seen first-hand the development of campaigning techniques on all sides.

I hope this experience of campaigning qualifies me to share some observations on how to win an election and the art of political campaigning. It *is* an art, not a science. You can read all the campaign textbooks you like, but experience, as Tony Benn once remarked, is the greatest teacher of all.

TO MY PARENTS

Part One

Planning and Preparation

1 What are Elections for?

Before embarking on an election campaign it is worth taking a moment to look at what elections are for, and how democracy, or more accurately democracies for there is more than a single definition, work.

Elections are the essential component of a democracy and what distinguishes democratic from non-democratic systems of government. Elections serve to elect representatives and confer upon them authority in the form of a democratic mandate. The election of representatives to a representative body also serves, in a party system, to determine the political control of that body. In parliamentary terms, we vote for our local MP as an individual candidate, but if enough MPs of the same party are elected from across the country, they will form the government of the country.

An election is the opportunity to make democracy work. It is the moment when all citizens of a country or locality have an equal say over who their representatives and government should be. The vote of an Internet millionaire counts the same as a *Big Issue* seller. It is the moment when the governed can change their governments, when politicians can be held to account, when the people – the *demos* – speak. Elections have been described as 'the feast of democracy'.

Elections are not just for Members of Parliament and to decide which party forms a government. We elect our local government councillors, our town or parish councillors, our Members of the European Parliament, our workplace representatives, our trade union officials, and if we are members, the officers of any one of a million clubs and societies. If we live in Scotland, Wales, Northern Ireland or London we can vote for our representatives in the various devolved assemblies established since 1997. Soon we may be able to elect members of the House of Lords. In the USA, the majority of public officials are elected, from the judges to the dog-catchers. But with falling turnouts, growing distrust and whole sections of society dislocated from elections, can the preponderance of elected officials at every level be equated with better democracy?

We can even vote for who should be evicted from *Big Brother* and who should win the *Stars in their Eyes* final. Unless uncontested, all of these elections involve election campaigns at a local, regional, and national level.

General elections

In the thirteenth century the monarch summoned a Parliament. The sheriff in each county was responsible for returning the names of those who would serve in the Parliament to the Sovereign – which is the origin of the title Returning Officer. Today, we have general elections to decide who forms the Parliament, although anyone watching a Queen's Speech, where the MPs are summoned to the House of Lords to hear the monarch tell them what 'her' government will do, may ponder on the role of the Crown in our parliamentary affairs.

General elections take place at least once every five years, barring war and national emergency. The exact timing within the five year Parliament is decided by the Prime Minister, using the powers of the royal prerogative, which means the Prime Minister can decide without reference to anyone else, including the Cabinet or Parliament. Getting the timing right is a political skill in itself. Too early – and people say you've cut and run; too late – and people think you're afraid of an election. The longer a parliament carries on, the likelihood increases of poor by-election results or unseen events buffeting your government. James Callaghan waited until 1979 and went through the public sector strikes of the Winter of Discontent, which might have been avoided if he had gone in 1978. His response to the clamour of those wanting to know when the election would be was to sing Marie Lloyd's 'Waiting at the Church' at the TUC Congress – possibly the most ill-advised example of public singing by a politician until Northern Ireland Secretary Peter Brooke sang 'Oh My Darling Clementine' on Irish TV. In September 2000 William Hague challenged Tony Blair to call an election straight away, even though the Parliament was only three years old.

Prime Ministers' calculations involve the state of the economy and especially the effect of tax rises or cuts, international events, and particularly those involving the British Armed Services, the opinion polls, and the state of the parties, especially if the parliamentary majority is small. They also weigh up the weather forecast, sporting events especially football, Royal birthdays and weddings, and any other factors which might influence the national mood. The PM will take advice from a variety of sources and colleagues, the newspapers will be full of speculation and double-guessing, but the decision of when to 'go to the country' rests with the Prime Minister alone.

This Prime Ministerial power to decide the date of the general election is a hangover from the days when British Monarchs ran the show and could decide whatever they wanted. Various royal prerogative powers have been passed to Prime Ministers to exercise on behalf of the Crown. There is a strong argument, as articulated by Neil Kinnock before the 1992 general election, for fixed-term parliaments. A parliament would last five years, unless a government could no longer rely on the confidence of the House of Commons, and everyone would be clear when the general election was coming. Fixed-term parliaments may take some of the fun out of politics, but they would help create a more sensible and stable platform for democracy.

General elections decide which party will form a government, and thus the direction of politics and the economy for the country. In this sense general elections create history, and you can play some interesting counter-factual games working out what would have happened if the results went the other way. If Margaret Thatcher had lost the 1979 general election and Labour had won it, her party would have deposed her within months and Thatcherism would have been stillborn. If Churchill had won in 1945, it is doubtful there would have been an NHS. If John Major hadn't won in 1992, it would have been Neil Kinnock's Labour Party which would have had to deal with the economic crisis and devaluation, prompting a chorus of 'I told you so' and consigning Labour to defeat in 1997.

There are times when general elections represent major moments in history and serve as a landmark. In 1906, 1945, 1979 and 1997 the general elections can be seen as clear changes in national mood and a change in direction. Other times, such as 1950, 1966, and both 1974 elections, the results are less clear. But it remains the case that general elections are the archetypal election campaigns where the latest techniques are tried and the skills of the electioneers are tested.

By-elections

If general elections are the feast of democracy, by-elections are the democratic snack you can enjoy between meals without ruining your appetite. They are caused when the existing sitting Member of Parliament is unable to continue as an MP, through death, resignation, or elevation to the House of Lords. Between May 1997 and the end of 2000 there were 17 by-elections in the UK:

Uxbridge
Paisley South
Beckenham
Winchester
Leeds Central
Eddisbury
Wigan
Hamilton South
Kensington and Chelsea
Ceredigion
Romsey
Tottenham
South Antrim
Preston
Glasgow Anniesland
West Bromwich West
and Falkirk West.

Ten were caused by the death of the sitting Member of Parliament, five were caused by resignation (including Betty Boothroyd, the Speaker), one was caused by George Robertson's elevation to the Lords to allow him to become Secretary General of NATO, and one – Winchester – was caused by the original general election result being called out of order.

Because by-elections are fought in between elections and are usually one-offs (although if there is more than one by-election pending they try to cluster them together), they assume huge importance to political parties and commentators. The results of by-elections are picked over for signs of swings and shifts in opinion, and for portents of what might happen in a general election. For governments they are a pain because they give voters the chance to give the government a kicking, without bringing it down. It is a low-risk way of expressing dissatisfaction. For opposition parties they represent the chance to create a big swing and possibly pick up another seat, which adds to their sense of momentum. For the Opposition, they offer the chance of electoral recovery.

For politicians, by-elections present an unexpected and welcome chance to get into the House of Commons without waiting for the general election to come around. When a senior politician loses their seat, by-elections are their chance to get back into the action. Tony Benn lost his Bristol seat in 1983, and was back by 1984 as the MP for Chesterfield. Michael Portillo lost his Enfield Southgate seat in 1997, but in 1999 won the Kensington and Chelsea by-election. It doesn't always work – Labour's Foreign Secretary, Patrick Gordon Walker, lost his seat in Smethwick in 1964 and attempted to re-enter Parliament in a by-election in January 1965 in Leyton. Despite this being a 'safe' Labour seat, local voters detected that they were being exploited, and he lost. Aspiring politicians wanting a seat in the House of Commons keep a discreet but watchful eye on the health of ailing MPs in safe seats.

By-elections represent intensive campaigning opportunities because parties can divert a higher level of resources than during a general election. The resources are not spread as thinly. Volunteers can be bussed in from all over the country, national party campaign staff can be parachuted into the constituency for weeks on end, direct mail can be used intensively, huge poster boards can be erected in people's front gardens. Some party staff, such as Labour's John Braggins, are acknowledged experts at by-election campaigning and can move into a constituency for weeks to run a campaign. By-elections are elections fought to the full, because the efforts are more concentrated and the stakes are high.

Local elections

In Britain, local government is largely the product of evolutionary development, punctuated by Acts of Parliament designed to tidy things up. This means that there is no unified structure of local democracy across the UK. In some parts of the country there is a single tier of local democracy – such as in London, in the big metropolitan areas like Manchester and Liverpool, and in Scotland and Wales. In other parts there are two layers of local council – the county council, and the district council, with distinct powers and duties. Councillors tend to serve four-year terms of office. Some councils elect their councillors 'by thirds' which means that one third of council seats are up for election every year. Other councils, such as in London, have elections for all seats at once, every four years.

Local government runs a range of services including education, social services, libraries and parks, street cleaning and emptying the bins, and serves as the focal point for local community activity and investment. There are still plenty of people who want to be councillors. Some want to serve their community, others see it as a way of advancing their political careers. Of the 183 new Labour MPs in 1997, two-thirds had been councillors. Of these, 80 were councillors in the constituency in which they went on to become MP.

Standing as a candidate in local elections involves many of the same activities as parliamentary elections – getting selected, running canvassing and doorstep work, producing leaflets and posters, and getting the vote out on polling day. The differences are that the geographical area is much smaller – a ward instead of a parliamentary constituency, which means you can knock on the door of every potential voter, and also you are one candidate amongst many. There may be more than one candidate from each party fighting in each ward, where there are multi-member seats.

Council by-elections can be caused between the fixed elections every four years by 'a casual vacancy' arising, through death or resignation.

The general pace and scale of local elections is slower and smaller than a general election or by-election. There is little media interest; turnout is smaller, and the results are less likely to be cataclysmic. But for the candidates who become councillors and for the people reliant on local government services, the results are all-important.

European elections

Elections for the European Parliament take place every four years throughout the ever-growing European Union, to uniform indifference from the great British public. Britain changed its system of European elections in 1999. Instead of Euro-MPs representing a single constituency, now the MEPs are elected by regions and more than one MEP represents each region. This involves a system of proportional representation and the regional list system.

The 1999 European elections were a low point in British democracy. There was widespread apathy about the purpose of the election and ignorance about the issues. The new system put many people off, because they felt they were no longer electing a personal representative, and because the voting system with its long ballot paper was deemed to be confusing. Ruth Turner was a candidate in the Euro-elections, and she says: 'Many in the media were reporting on the "confusing ballot paper" before they'd even seen it, and that must have put some people off. In fact, the ballot paper was easy to follow because all you had to do was vote for the party you wanted to support.'

Turnout fell to below a quarter of the electorate.

The devolved assemblies

One of the lasting legacies of the Labour Government elected in 1997 is a new tier of government for Scotland, Wales, Northern Ireland and - London. The Scottish Parliament, the Welsh Assembly, the Northern Ireland Assembly and the Greater London Assembly are up and working, and represent either the rebirth of democracy, or the break-up of the United Kingdom depending on your view. All these assemblies certainly mean more election campaigns and more candidates.

The Scottish Parliament has 129 members; 73 are elected from a constituency, and 56 are additional members elected using proportional representation within the European constituencies. In Wales, the Assembly contains 60 elected members. Forty are from constituencies, and 20 are elected using the Additional Member System from the five European constituencies. The Northern Ireland Assembly has 108 elected members, with each Westminster parliamentary constituency electing six members.

In London, the furore in 2000 over Ken Livingstone's defection from the Labour Party to stand as an independent candidate for Mayor for London masked the creation of the Greater London Assembly and the election of 25 Assembly Members - 14 from constituencies and 11 as top-up members elected under the Additional Member System. New systems of elections have thrown up their own challenges. With AMS systems, people can vote twice, creating opportunities for tactical second-place voting and 'split-ticket' voting. In the London elections only one in twenty voters exercised their second place vote in the same way as their first one.

The new system of counting votes caused some problems too. The new electronic vote counting systems were slowed down by static electricity caused by the traditional baize table-covers and the plastic ballot-boxes. Counts went on for hours longer than a traditional count, and with no piles of votes being counted by hand, there was nothing to see.

Barry Quirk, Returning Officer for the Lewisham and Greenwich GLA constituency, says that the new systems may be more efficient but 'the count was totally tedious for agents and candidates. There was no drama. I got some CDs from my car to play to the campaign teams during the count. In the end I sent them all home, and woke them up by phone in the morning to get them to come back for the result.'

The problems with democracy

The reality is that our systems of democracy are flawed, and what actually happens falls far short of the ideal. There are four main areas of concern:

- voter switch-off
- dumbing down
- the crooked electoral system
- the democratic deficit

Voter switch-off

First, despite the extension of the vote to virtually all the adult population, not everyone votes. In most elections, not even a majority of the electorate votes. Turnouts – the number of people turning out to vote – in recent European and local government elections have fallen to below a quarter. On June 10 1999, at the Leeds Central by-election, just 19.6 per cent of the electorate came out to vote for their new MP. In the European elections held on the same day, the national turnout was 23.3 per cent. At one polling station in Sunderland, just 15 people out of a possible 1000 voted. Tony Blair's famous victory in 1997 was based on the lowest turnout in a general election since 1935. In 1950, 84 per cent of the electorate voted. In 1997, just 71 per cent.

In November 2000, three by-elections took place which confirmed the sad pattern. Despite the rash of media coverage and campaign visits by everyone from Tony Blair to former Eastenders actor Ross Kemp, in West Bromwich West, turnout was 27.6 per cent; in Preston, it was 29.4 per cent, and in Glasgow Anniesland it was 38.42 per cent. As pollster Anthony King commented at the time 'turnout was derisory'.

In the USA, which often presages political developments here, turnouts are even more derisory. In 1980, half those voters aged under 35 voted; in 1996 the figure was only 39 per cent.

So representatives are being elected, and governments decided, by a decreasing number of people. For example, the three new Labour MPs elected on 23 November 2000, Adrian Bailey, Mark Hendrick, and John Robertson had only 9,640, 9,765 and 10,539 votes each, but their predecessors had double, or triple, that number. This has two effects – first that councillors and MPs become less representative, and second that increasing numbers of people are disenfranchised from the democratic system. But it is worse even than that – because turnouts do not fall evenly amongst all social groups. Those staying at home instead of voting are more likely to be working-class than middle class. We have a long way to go before involvement in the electoral system becomes as divided along lines of race and income as the USA, but we can discern the start of the same process. Politics in Britain is becoming increasingly the language of the educated, salaried, middle class. This has led some, for example Mark Tami and Tom Watson in a 1999 Fabian Society pamphlet, to suggest that Britain follows the Australian example and makes voting compulsory.

Dumbing down

Second, not everyone votes on the basis of the same amount of information. People are largely making their electoral choices in a state of blissful ignorance. Voters do not attend political meetings, or read manifestos or election addresses. Politics is being dumbed down to the extent where political illiteracy is the norm. There is a story of a doorstep exchange told by the former MP for Harrow East, Hugh Dykes, which exemplifies the point:

Voter: 'I'm not too keen on Europe. In fact I don't think we should join the Community at all.'

Hugh Dykes: 'But we joined in 1973.'
Voter: 'No, dear, get your facts right. That was the Common-
                      wealth.'

Unlike many countries, Britain does not teach citizenship in our schools. The newspapers reduce politics to personalities and gladiatorial combats between leaders, and the broadcaster distil politics into 15-second soundbites. The media tends to concentrate on trivia rather than serious debate, which leads politicians to steer away from serious debate in favour of whatever will get them headlines. Parliament, apart from the absurd spectacle of Prime Ministers' Questions, is reported less and less by the media. The big issues are swept aside in favour of political tittle-tattle and rumour.

When Tony Blair made his speech to the Labour Party conference in 2000, most newspapers focused on the fact that he had got hot and sweaty making the speech, not the ideas and policies it contained.

The crooked electoral system

Third, the British electoral system, known as 'first-past-the-post', means that general elections throw up skewed electoral results. A majority of the electorate voted against the Conservatives throughout the 1980s and 1990s yet they won a majority of the seats. In 1951, Labour won a majority of the votes, and more votes than in 1945, but lost the election. The Tories won 250,000 fewer votes than Labour, but won a majority of 17 seats. 1951 stands as Labour's best result ever. After six years of establishing the National Health Service, nationalising the mines and railways, giving independence to India and moving to a peacetime economy, more people than ever before or since voted Labour. But the Conservatives won because of the crooked electoral system.

In Scotland and in Wales, millions of people vote Conservative, but there are no Scottish or Welsh Conservative MPs at all. Throughout the South of England there are areas with no Labour MPs. So in these cases the role of elections to choose representatives does not work. A Conservative in Scotland has no direct representation for their views. A Labour voter in South Buckinghamshire is in the same boat.

First-past-the-post delivers governments with majorities on the basis of a minority of the votes. In 1978, Lord Hailsham spoke of an 'elective dictatorship' to describe the phenomenon of parties with minorities of the vote enjoying majorities of the seats in the House of Commons. He was referring to the Labour Government of James Callaghan, but the majority of voters voted against Margaret Thatcher throughout the eighties, yet she won three elections in a row. Those in favour of first-past-the-post argue that the system delivers strong governance. But even under this system, Britain has been governed by coalition governments for 43 of the past 150 years, such as the Unionist coalition of 1895-1905 and the Churchill Government of 1940-1945, and 34 years when the governing party relied on the votes of another party, or parties, such as James Callaghan's Government in 1976-1979. So for 77 years out of 150, first-past-the-post has delivered coalitions and unstable governments.

First-past-the-post works at the local level to skew the results of local council elections. Many councils are virtually one-party states although other parties receive sizeable numbers of votes, because the number of council seats does not reflect the proportion of the votes received. In local government first-past-the-post delivers not strong administrations but arrogant, unaccountable, lazy and unchallenged majority groups.

The democratic deficit

Fourth, much power in Britain is exercised by undemocratic, unelected individuals and bodies. The Conservative Governments in the 1980s did much to centralise the state and remove decision-making from democratic to non-democratic bodies. The great symbol of what Simon Jenkins has called the 'nationalisation of Britain' was the abolition of the Greater London Council (GLC) in 1986 despite a campaign to stop them, led by its leader, Ken Livingstone. I wonder whatever happened to him. This period saw the growth of the Quango (the Quasi-Autonomous Non-Governmental Organisation). Decisions which affect our lives, across health, education, the law, and local services, are being taken by people who are unelected and unaccountable. This failing of the system is known as the 'democratic deficit.'

These four dilemmas for democracy – falling turnout and levels of participation, the dumbing down of political debate, the unfair election system, and the democratic deficit – all contribute to the gradual erosion of democracy. On the housing estates and in the inner-cities, democracy is ending, not with a bang, but a whimper. If democracy in Britain fails, it won't be because of *coup d'etat*. There'll be no revolutionary soviets or troops in the streets, no capture of the radio stations and martial law. It will die because we couldn't be bothered to save it.

The prospects for democracy

'As I would not be a slave, so I would not be a master. This expresses my idea of democracy.'

Abraham Lincoln

Democracy is an impressively durable system, and it can be applied in virtually any political situation anywhere in the world. Within our own times we have seen the spread of democracy to the countries of the former Soviet Union and to South Africa. In the former Yugoslavia, democracy has forced out dictators. Watching black South Africans queue for hours to cast their first post-apartheid vote in 1994 was an inspiration, and served to make us treasure our own democracy no matter how flawed.

It is, as Winston Churchill said 'the worst form of government except for all the other forms that have been tried.'

Democracy must evolve as times change, and find new ways to put its principles into practice. It must be about more than casting a vote every few years. It should be about an active, engaged citizenry working with governments and representatives all year round to help them take representative decisions. Here the Internet will play a central role. The Internet has already transformed the way we work, shop and play. The Internet will transform politics too. The way we have access to information, the way we can communicate with our representatives, the way we can be asked for our views through online polling and referenda, and ultimately the way we vote, will become dependent on the Internet. The Democratic Party in Arizona, USA made history in 2000 by setting up Internet-based voting for the state's presidential primary. More than 35,000 voters – a third of the eligible electorate – voted for their choice of candidate to fight the US presidential election. 'This is a quicker, faster, easier way to vote than we've ever had in the United States,' said state party chairman Mark Fleisher.

Dick Morris, the American political strategist and former adviser to Bill Clinton, sees the role of the Internet as transforming the type of democracy in the USA. His case is that for the first time since the early nineteenth century, the United States is moving from a Madisonian model of representative democracy towards a Jeffersonian model of direct democracy. In other words indirect democracy, whereby we elect people to take decisions on our behalf and hope that they do the right thing is being superseded by direct democracy whereby our views can be instantly aggregated and implemented via technology. This direct democracy is in theory a purer form of democracy. Morris says 'what small size and intimate geography permitted ancient Athens to accomplish, the Internet will let America and the world accomplish.'

In a similar vein, Andrew Adonis and Geoff Mulgan, both now working for Tony Blair at Number Ten, have written 'Back to Greece' – an essay about the scope for direct democracy using referenda, citizens' juries and panels, and electronic voting on issues and for candidates. So as far as the future of democracy is concerned, Greece is the word.

This is an appealing notion, but we should be careful not to ascribe the Internet with too many transformational powers. Remember they said that television would lead to a new Enlightenment, but that was before *Neighbours from Hell* and *Top Gear*. For Tony Benn, in 1958, 'television is the greatest, best and most important thing that has happened in British politics.'

Many people still do not have access to the Internet, although access will become as common as owning a television within a few years. The main concern should be that if political decision-making can be reduced to clicking a mouse, will decisions be any better? If governments were subject to instant recall, we would have more governments than Italy. Whenever a government pursued an unpopular but correct policy, it would be booted out of office. Governments would simply pursue the popular, at the expense of long-term interests. There is a need for established 'terms of office' when administrations can do their job. Even the Chartists thought the terms of office for governments should be twelve months.

Beating apathy

There have been various attempts to stir up interest in elections. A Home Office working party in 2000 recommended the following variations:

- Polling hours: variations in polling hours to allow different start or finish times.
- Polling days: moving polling to an alternative weekday or a day at the weekend or allowing voting over more than one day.
- Early voting: opening a limited number of polling stations in the period before polling day at accessible locations to allow any eligible elector to vote.
- Mobile polling: providing a mobile polling station which could take the ballot box to groups of voters, for example, by visiting residential and convalescent homes.
- Out of area voting: allowing electors to vote at any polling station in the electoral area, or even outside it.
- All postal ballots: allowing an election to be held on the basis of postal voting only.
- Electronic voting: supplementing polling booths and polling stations with automated voting equipment, telephone voting or online remote voting via the Internet.

In the 2000 local elections, 32 areas experimented with different types of voting, including early voting in Blackburn, Blackpool, Chester, Coventry, postal voting in Doncaster, Wigan and Gateshead, extension of voting hours in Leeds, Milton Keynes and Mole Valley, electronic voting in Three Rivers, Salford and Stevenage, and a mobile ballot box in Watford. Some areas experimented with combinations of changes. The results showed that although the schemes made voting easier and were appreciated by those voters who took part, they did little to increase turnout.

The answers will lie not in making technical adjustments to the timing and places of voting, but the incentives and rationale for voting in the first place. As Ralph Nader has said 'there can be no daily democracy without daily citizenship.' We need a new definition of democracy, which extends beyond the old notion that a citizen with a vote every few years equals democracy. Democracy must be a daily practice, in a society where people are being asked their views and being listened to by the people whose decisions will affect them. That might mean more citizens' juries and panels, where people get to take part in deliberative and long-term decision-making about local issues and services.

Wherever power lies and decisions are taken, democracy must be allowed to work.

It might mean that politicians listen to voters more via online surgeries and virtual hustings. It might mean that companies and retailers involve their customers in decisions about their neighbourhoods. It might mean more worker participation in management decisions. It might mean all of these things, and more. Democratising all aspects of our lives will lead to a deeper, multi-dimensional system of democratic participation. But there will always be elections and winning elections is what this book is all about.

How much difference does the campaign make?

Political choices are made by voters based on more than the few weeks of a general election or local election campaign. Neil Kinnock famously said that 'elections are won in years, not weeks.' Voters decide who to vote for based on a range of factors, and the campaign serves to remind people to vote and to reawaken whatever views on politics they may have formulated over the previous years.

If a government is widely perceived to have failed in office or not delivered on its promises, even the best campaign will not save it. If John Major's campaign in 1997 had been utterly brilliant and he had promised to abolish income tax and give everyone a new car, he would still have lost because his government had lost the trust of many of its former supporters. Some argue that the 1997 general election was lost on 16 September 1992, when Britain was ejected from the Exchange Rate Mechanism and the government was forced into a humiliating devaluation of the pound. Major's Government was on the defensive from that moment on, and as its troubles mounted over the next four years, the result of the next general election looked increasingly clear. The campaign had little impact. One defeated Conservative MP said afterwards 'my result would have been exactly the same if I had spent six weeks in the South of France.'

Oppositions can lose elections by their behaviour too. In 1983, Labour asked the electorate for support after four years of internal warfare, a damaging Deputy Leadership contest, the breakaway by the SDP, and recent memories of the 'Winter of Discontent' still vivid. Labour's campaign was a shambles, but the previous four years' disarray had done more to seal Labour's crushing defeat in 1983 than a poorly organised campaign.

Some academics, commentators and even politicians see election campaigns as mere ritual, with little impact on voting behaviour. For example, after Labour's 1959 defeat, Anthony Crosland wrote 'the élan of the rank and file is less and less essential to the winning of elections. With the growing penetration of the mass media, political campaigning has become increasingly centralised; and the traditional local activities, the door-to-door canvassing and the rest, are now largely a ritual.'

Analyst David Butler echoes this idea of campaign-as-ritual. He says: 'the campaign may to some extent be a ritual dance, a three-week repetition of well-aired themes, making no substantial net difference to the outcome. British elections are usually won over the long haul. A very large proportion of people vote out of team loyalty, supporting the party that they – and their parents too – have always supported; those that change their minds are usually converted, not because of the final three weeks, but over months and years because of an accumulated impression, positive or negative, of the values and the performance of rival parties.'

But if campaigns don't make much difference then why do parties spend so much time and effort engaging in them? In 1997, the parties spent roughly one pound for every person in Britain. Could they have saved their money?

To the relief of election campaigners everywhere, there has been new evidence which proves what we all hoped – that local election campaigns in the community do make a difference, albeit small, to the outcome of elections. Campaign activities such as street stalls, membership drives, knocking on doors, telephone canvassing, distribution of leaflets and so on have been proved, notably by two sets of academics, Seyd and Whiteley, and Denver and Hands, to have an effect on the outcome of elections. It may seem like common sense that a political party with a strong local presence, a high level of local members in the community, an attractive and plausible candidate, and a slick canvassing and getting-out-the-vote operation will do better than one reliant on national media coverage without a local base. Election campaigns which rely on purely national efforts, such as the expensive Referendum Party campaign in 1997 bankrolled by James Goldsmith, lose out because of the lack of a local activist base.

Butler and Kavanagh, the election analysts, say: 'In 1997, the Labour Party brought to an altogether new pitch the sophisticated presentation of its messages nationally and locally. The six weeks of the campaign did not, of course, decide the outcome, but the three years of disciplined preparation and the final assault must have had a substantial impact on the scale of the majority.'

Academics have proved that the activist base is worth 1000–2000 votes in each constituency. The effects may be marginal, but so is the majority in scores of parliamentary seats, and in some years such as 1950, 1964, and 1992, the overall outcome of an election, and the formation of government, was dependent on the outcome in a handful of seats. So marginal it may be, but campaigning does make a difference.

2   The Nine Tribes of Politics

Politics is a minority sport. The consequences of political action affect everyone. No one is untouched by the actions of government, Europe or local councils. Yet, only a minority of the population is actively involved at any level of politics, beyond casting a vote every few years or so.

Those that are so are mostly involved through local political party branches, which exist at the level of the local town or local council ward, and in Britain consist of the main parties – Labour, Tory and Liberal Democrat, and the nationalist parties in Scotland and Wales (Plaid Cymru and the Scottish Nationalists). In Northern Ireland the political parties reflect the sectarian divide in that troubled Province. These activists are often local councillors and local office-holders, and run local elections, stand as candidates in elections, and run the activities of the local branch or unit.

The next level of involvement is elected office itself. Here we find politicians, who are most obvious manifestation of politics. But they are the tip of the iceberg. Around politicians cluster the various camp-followers of politics – the advisers and counsellors, the assistants and researchers, who enable politicians to function. Each national party headquarters has its own dedicated team of staffers. In Government and Opposition, there are Special Advisors to help front bench politicians with their departmental responsibilities and deal with the media. And then there are the people who make a living out of politics, not by standing for office or following a particular party, but by reporting, analysing and commentating on politics.

Some of the people in politics are unsung heroes. Some of the people in politics are very odd indeed. As with any *milieu*, there are distinct personality types and tribes which inhabit the world of politics. In order to better understand election campaigns, and at the risk of offending a great deal of people I know, I have tried to identify and characterise the *dramatis personae* of the political drama.

They are:
- voters
- candidates
- activists
- fixers
- spin doctors
- pollsters
- pundits
- policy wonks
- journalists

Each group has its own function, characteristics and culture, and its own tribal loyalties and ritual. These, then, are the nine tribes of politics.

Voters

You can't have an election without voters. Sometimes our political leaders may wish that you could, but you can't. Political parties spend a lot of time and effort trying to work out what the voters think and what they want. They try canvassing, opinion-polling, surveys and focus groups and knocking on doors to talk to as many as possible. Yet the ungrateful voters' response is usually that politicians are all out of touch, and you never see them apart from at election time. The relationship is a strange not to say strained one. Voters complain that politicians don't listen, but when an eager candidate knocks on their door during *Coronation Street* or the finals of the World Cup, they don't like it.

The size of the electorate has grown over the past two hundred years as the result of campaigns to extend the franchise to new groups of society. Before the 1832 Great Reform Act only five per cent of the adult population had the vote. But after it this dramatically increased to a whopping seven per cent. There has always been hostility to the idea of extending the vote beyond the rich. In 1852, the Conservative Prime Minister Benjamin Disraeli said 'I doubt very much whether a democracy is a government that would suit this country.' In 1866 he stated that an extension of the franchise would lead to a Parliament filled with 'a horde of selfish and obscure mediocrities, incapable of anything but mischief'. So at least he was right about one thing.

Further Reform Acts in 1867 and 1884 extended the vote to 16 and then 28 per cent of adults. The real breakthrough came when women were given the vote (or when they took it, to be more accurate) in 1918, but it was not until 1928 that virtually all men and women over 21 had the vote. Harold Wilson lowered the voting age to 18 in 1969. Like most of British history, our reputation as a bastion of democracy and the Mother of Parliaments is something of a fraud. Some would argue that Britain is still only a half-grown democracy while there is hereditary monarchy, hereditary members of the House of Lords, and the unfair first-past-the-post system.

Politics in Britain has been characterised by the breakdown in voters' loyalties to parties – dubbed 'voter dealignment'.

At the height of the Victorian era Gilbert and Sullivan could claim in *Iolanthe* that:

Nature always doth contrive
That every boy and every gal
Who's born into the world alive
Is either a little Liberal
Or else a little Conserv-a-tive.

In the first half of the twentieth century, Labour replaced the Liberals as the main party of the industrial and urban areas, and the two-party system reasserted itself. You could tell, nine times out of ten, whether a person was a Tory or Labour by what they looked like, the street they lived in, the job they did, and their accent.

John O'Farrell recalls: 'You can usually tell how someone votes before they come to the front door. Immaculately swept front steps, well-trimmed hedges and a mud-splattered Range Rover parked in the drive with a sticker saying "I slow down for fox hunters" do not augur well for a Labour canvasser.'

Since the 1960s, changes in society and the economy have meant that voters behave less like social blocks and more like individual consumers. These days you are less likely to be able to tell how someone votes from his or her social class or occupation. They have become discerning and vote on a case-by-case basis. There are still those who are Labour, Liberal or Tory because of family attachment or for cultural or historical reasons, or even for ideological reasons. But the old tribal following of either party has gone forever. In 1964, 43 per cent of voters 'identified strongly' with either Labour or Tories. In 1979 it was down to 26 per cent. In 1992, the figure had fallen to below 20 per cent. The voters are a fickle bunch.

Candidates

If you are considering whether to stand for office, the first question you must ask is 'Are you absolutely sure?' Modern politics is a tough, unfair, exhausting and grubby pursuit. It leaves no time for a decent family life or friends and pastimes. Local councillors are elected on a wave of optimism and public-minded enthusiasm, and slowly over their four-year terms are worn down by an endless round of committee meetings and ward surgeries. They join the council to improve the lives of the people in their area, but most are consigned to the scrutiny committee on refuse collection and street cleansing.

At Westminster, politicians fare little better. The pressures are enormous, the hours exhausting, the reward little and the thanks non-existent. The incidence of divorce, alcohol-abuse and mental illness is high. Political advancement is slow, if it comes at all. The benches of Westminster are littered with bitter men and women passed over for promotion or sacked from office who believe they deserve better. At the end of thirty or forty years' service, even the most successful of politicians can expect to end their days flogging memoirs, appearing on political documentaries, giving after-dinner speeches, or simply dropping down dead. It doesn't sound terribly appealing, does it?

If you put yourself forward for election, the first thing to disappear is your private life. Politicians can expect every detail of their lives and their families' lives to be unearthed and dissected. Characters like 'Benjy the Bin Man' – and he's not the only one at this game – go through politicians' rubbish bins in search of incriminating evidence. Embarrassing relatives will become minor celebrities. School friends and University acquaintances, former lovers and business partners will eagerly sell their stories and worse, their embarrassing photographs, to the newspapers. The spliffs you may have shared, the rum and cokes you drank on your eighteenth birthday, the college dalliances, the membership of CND or the

Monday Club – if your political career rises above the very lowest of the rungs on the ladder, the truth will out.

It was Aristotle who suggested that democracy would only work if everyone who wanted to stand for office was immediately disqualified, and maybe he had a point.

Some people are not allowed to be candidates. Foreigners, under-21s, Peers of the Realm, Roman Catholic or Church of England clergy (although this is set to change thanks to the efforts of Siobhan McDonagh MP), the mentally ill, bankrupts, those who have committed electoral fraud, people in prison, those found guilty of treason, civil servants, the police and Armed Forces are disbarred from standing as a candidate.

Anyone else, if driven to it, may stand.

In an election the candidate is the lynchpin. They must be unfailingly cheerful. They must never lose their tempers, or raise their voices. They must be always grateful to party workers, and never tired or grumpy. Even if their campaign, and their career is going down the toilet, they must never let their feelings show. Candidates must possess super-human reserves of happiness, energy, gratitude, interest in others, and gregariousness.

As a former US Congressman put it: 'one must have the friendliness of a child, the enthusiasm of a teenager, the assurance of a college boy, the diplomacy of a wayward husband, the curiosity of a cat, and the good humour of an idiot.'

Candidates think they are most important part of an election, although behind their backs agents describe them as merely a 'legal necessity'. Some candidates, especially established politicians, are prone to an inflated sense of their own importance. But candidates should be humbled by the thought that most people are voting for parties not individuals, and even the most established politician can be ousted as the result of national swings and national party fortunes. It is not their dazzling brilliance and insight that people are voting for, it is the colour of their rosette. Just ask Marcus Fox, the ousted MP for Shipley. As Chairman of the 1922 Committee, Marcus Fox was the epitome of the Tory grandee. During many decades as the MP for Shipley, Fox must have met virtually every constituent in person, and was well known locally. He had kept his nose clean and been untroubled by the sleaze which had engulfed so many of his colleagues. Yet he lost his seat to an unknown Labour candidate, Chris Leslie, whose previous contribution to politics was to do Gordon Brown's photocopying, because of the national swing from Tory to Labour. Marcus Fox's professional merits and his personal support wasn't enough to keep him in his job.

Activists

Activists, and the clue is in the name, are those active in support of a political party or a political cause. Activists are the people who are members of local branches of their chosen political party, and who perform the functions necessary to the working of democracy at a constituency or ward level.

Activists attend party meetings, they discuss issues of local and national concern, they organise events to raise funds such as jumble sales, coffee mornings and cheese and wine parties, they may hold office such as party chairman or treasurer, they run the committee rooms during elections and organise the canvassing and campaigning and they provide a pool of potential candidates for council or parliamentary elections. They knock on doors canvassing and deliver leaflets in all weathers, they staff street stalls and attend meetings, and, without thanks and with little reward, they keep democracy going. After police-dog handlers and postmen, political activists probably have the highest incidence of dog bites of any social group. They venture into corners of Britain where the light seldom shines, and knock on doors which no-one else notices.

The nature of local political parties and the fact that only a small number of people are interested, means that activists end up doing most of the tasks outlined above. It is very difficult to be a part-time activist. Once hooked, you can easily find yourself at one or two meetings a week, with endless hours spent engaging in political campaigns and administration. Political parties are like icebergs – the bit you see, in the shape of local activists, is only one-tenth of the total membership, with nine-tenths submerged and out of view. This means that political parties are run by hyper-activists, who have to fulfil a range of functions: personnel manager, accountant, diplomat, PR expert, copywriter, salesman, fundraiser and policy expert.

This problem of hyper-activism, with not enough hands to do all the jobs, is made worse by falling levels of activism and membership. The

Sheffield academics Paul Whiteley and Patrick Seyd have shown that the falling memberships of parties is matched by a falling level of activism within parties.

Many activists are decent, public-spirited individuals, who are concerned about their communities and want to express their values through political action. Active members of political parties also tend to be active magistrates or school governors or charity volunteers. In these people can be found true civic virtue and community spirit. It must be said, though, that some political activists can border on the obsessive, the cranky, the eccentric and the egotistical.

Some attend local party meetings because they like the sound of their own voice, and the chance to hear it gives them a moment in the week when they can feel important. No matter what subject is under discussion – macro-economics, globalisation, Aids, secondary education, the national health service, the Balkans, European monetary union – they have a view and want to share it with anyone within earshot. Others are obsessed by single issues, often quite obscure, and are blind to the disinterest of others. It is the job of a good chair of the meeting to keep them in order.

The problem is not new. Sidney Webb, the leading socialist, wrote a hundred years ago that local Labour parties 'were frequently unrepresentative groups of nonentities dominated by fanatics, cranks and extremists.' George Orwell's view was that left-wing activists consisted of 'every fruit-juice drinker, nudist, sandal-wearer, sex-maniac, Quaker, 'nature-cure' quack, pacifist and feminist in England.'

The best account of life as an activist is John O'Farrell's *Things Can Only Get Better* which is an affectionate reminiscence of life in the Labour Party between 1979 and 1997, when Labour was in Opposition and tended to lose all the time. O'Farrell describes the camaraderie and friendship of life on the losing side, but the book also proves the futility of so much local activism.

Leonard Woolf, Labour activist and husband of Virginia, looked back over his life in politics and made the same judgement as O'Farrell: 'Looking back at the age of eighty-eight over the fifty-seven years of my political work in England, knowing what I aimed at and the results, I see clearly that I achieved practically nothing. The world today and the history of the human ant-hill during the past fifty-seven years would be exactly the same as it is if I had played ping-pong instead of sitting on committees and writing books and memoranda. I have therefore to make the rather ignominious confession ... that I must have in a long life ground through between 150,000 and 200,000 hours of perfectly useless work.'

Leo McKinstry is a journalist and author who left politics in a state of disgust. After years of constituency activism he could take it no longer, and wrote a splenetic book *Fit to Govern?* about his experiences. He said 'For more than a decade, the Labour Party was my whole life. As a local activist I would spend hours delivering unwanted leaflets and writing unread newsletters. Every month brought a round of meetings. The world kept revolving on its axis and I kept attending meetings. No decisions of any importance were taken and most of the discussions were breathtakingly boring. Yet, through a sense of duty and guilt I kept on going, punishing myself like a Scandinavian being beaten with twigs in an overactive sauna.'

All political parties recognise the need to reform their structures and culture to put an end to experiences like these. Political parties need local activists to fight elections, raise money and serve as local advocates. A national party can only be national if it has active members all over the country. The nature of the British electoral system means that parties can be elected to government without balanced geographical representation, and that can be an unfortunate factor in the actions of government. Margaret Thatcher showed what she thought of Scotland, where the Tories had only a handful of MPs, by giving them the Poll Tax a whole year before anyone else. Countryside campaigners complain that New Labour, predominately a creature of the cities and conurbations, has no sympathy for rural life. For parties to be representative, and in tune with all strands of life and disparate communities, they need local activists drawn from those communities.

The tragedy of so much local political activity is that it is pointless. The ratio of stultifying, inefficient and routine bureaucracy to the recruiting, campaigning and electioneering which can make a difference, must be about ten to one. There is also the ever-present danger of activist burn-out, where people simply cannot take any more, reclaim their weekends and evenings, and drop out of activity for ever.

Fixers

Every politician needs a fixer. There are many jobs in politics which the politician him or herself cannot possibly engage in for reasons of probity, morality, or legality. The fixer is therefore a trusted lieutenant who fixes things. If the acres of text written about Bill Clinton are to be believed, his fixers, usually his State Trooper bodyguards, spent most of their time arranging for Clinton to meet young ladies in hotel rooms. Many American politicians have succumbed to the temptations of sex and drugs (Rock 'n' Roll is okay) and their fixers have been assigned in procuring quantities of both, and clearing up the mess afterwards.

In Britain, of course, no politician would have need for such services, except possibly for the Tory front bench who are all as high as kites if the newspapers are to be trusted. The machinations of the Tory Chief Whip Francis Urquhart in *House of Cards*, who cheated, lied and murdered his way to the top, remain the stuff of fiction.

But there are plenty of unsavoury political tasks which need fixing. Dropping people from a great height, ratting on deals, leaking documents to the media, liaison with big-money donors, negotiating with the opposition (inside and outside your own party): these dirty jobs need doing. The fixer can be a member of party staff, part of the politician's private office, or a more junior politician. They allow the political leader to rise above the fray, keep their hands clean of the dirty stuff of politics.

Spin doctors

'Spin doctor' has become a term of abuse in political discourse. It is spat out as the reason for all the ills of modern politics. The phrase's etymology doesn't help. As an amalgam of 'spin', as in the spin put on a ball in baseball to make it trick the hitter, and 'doctor' as in 'doctoring the facts', the term reeks of insincerity and underhand activity.

When asked what is wrong with politics, most people will cite 'spin' as a major culprit, by which they mean a lack of plain talk, honest dealings and speaking the truth. A recent survey showed that people defined 'spin doctor' as a 'liar', 'charlatan' and 'con artist'.

Although the phrase 'spin doctor' appeared only as recently as 1984 and originated in the United States, the practice it describes is much older. From the time the media began to influence the outcome of elections, politicians have needed to communicate to media owners, editors and journalists. That need created the Press Officer, Media Relations Officer, PR adviser and ultimately spin doctor. Politicians of all hues have employed the services of these experts in presentation and dealing with the media. Harold Wilson relied on Joe Haines, Margaret Thatcher had Bernard Ingham, Bill Clinton had George Stephanopolous. In the late nineties, coverage of British politics was dominated by stories about Spin doctors. Labour's spinners – Derek Draper, Charlie Whelan and Alastair Campbell – were in the media more than most MPs. Instead of spinning the story, they *became* the story. And when that happens, as Charlie Whelan found out, the only option is to walk.

Spin doctors work to give the media favourable information and interpretation of the facts on behalf of their political bosses. They work to point out the weaknesses in their opponents' case. They work in an environment of rolling 24-hour news, where political careers and parties' fortunes can be made and broken in minutes. Spin doctors are tactical, not strategic, weapons. They engage in hand-to-hand combat, fighting with journalists over every headline and bulletin. They are obsessive, restless, hyper-energetic. Their mobile phones are extensions of their personality, their pagers are seldom silent. They can be rude, boisterous, and combative to the new reporter or the journalist who failed to swallow their line, or else cajoling, flattering, charming to the editor or senior reporter on whom they are relying for a favourable slant.

Spin doctors exist because the media in modern democracies has become the main influencer on voter behaviour. Reality is subsumed by perception. Crime may be falling, but do people feel safer? Taxes may be rising, but do people think they've been cut? Immigration may be at the lowest rate for decades, but is that what people believe? The way to influence these perceptions, and therefore to win electoral support, is via the media. In the gap between reality and perception stands the spin doctor, ready to mould opinion and interpretation.

Their tools are both the rapier and the sledge-hammer. Some stories placed in the newspapers are the result of clever deals or double-bluffs; others are the result of bullying and bluster. The techniques of spin are myriad, as we shall see, but the true artists of spin can be counted on the fingers of one hand. Their characteristics include an utter loyalty to their political master and their cause, a detailed knowledge of the media, usually gleaned from first-hand experience, and confidence backed by the belief in their own invincibility. In the continual battle of wits, they believe they can win.

The really successful spin doctors are the ones you've never heard of, because part of the role is staying out of sight. Who can name Charlie Whelan's successor at the Treasury? The fact that you can't is a sign of his success. For decades the existence of a Prime Minister's spokesperson was officially denied, and what they told journalists was hidden behind phrases such as 'sources close to the Prime Minister' or 'Number Ten Officials'. Only under the current Labour Government has the Prime Minister's Official Spokesperson (or PMOS) become a recognised job, with transcripts of their twice-weekly briefings to journalists available on the Internet.

But the real genius belongs to those spin doctors who have persuaded us they are not spin doctors. Ken Livingstone stands as the prime example. Ken Livingstone is the King of Spin, the spin doctors' spin doctor, capable of manipulating the media and moulding public opinion while all the while maintaining his image as the underdog and man of the people. He won an election for London Mayor in May 2000, without any campaign on the ground, through the cunning strategic use of spin. Yet like the Devil, whose greatest achievement was to persuade us he doesn't exist, Ken Livingstone can play the innocent and join in the chorus of condemnation against the spin doctors.

Pollsters

Pollsters are the modern-day high priests of an election. Instead of cutting up chickens, they foretell the future by researching the attitudes, aspirations, and voting intentions of samples of the public. Political parties employ their services to help decide policy and strategy. MORI's Bob Worcester has been helping political parties, mostly Labour, since the days of Harold Wilson. Others, such as Greg Cook who was New Labour's pollster during the 1997 general election, are newer on the scene. Svengali-like figures such as Labour's Philip Gould have built their reputations on their hotlines to the electorate. By conducting polling, either surveys of a statistically-significant number of voters, or focus groups of small numbers, pollsters can tell politicians what the electorate are thinking. This is highly valuable information.

It is not always acted on, of course. In Labour's days of 'no compromise with the electorate', polling was viewed as another distasteful activity from the private sector along with advertising and public relations. In 1983, Bob Worcester would explain that Labour's defence policy was desperately unpopular, that the party's economic plans were viewed with suspicion and fear, and that people felt Labour was out of touch and extreme. But he was ignored by politicians who thought they knew best because the cheering crowds of supporters at the latest CND rally told them so.

Even as late as the 1990s, some elements of the pollster's arts were distrusted by politicians. Philip Gould remembers that key figures such as Alastair Campbell and Bruce Grocott MP (Blair's PPS) were highly sceptical about focus groups until they attended one.

So, by asking people what they think, through various methods, pollsters can discover what people are thinking about politics and let politicians act on their advice. As the electorate becomes ever more fickle, and public opinion becomes ever more tempestuous, the influence of the pollster will grow at the heart of British politics.

Pundits

Pundits usually fall into one of three categories: over-the-hill journalist, failed politician, or trendy academic. Pundits are wheeled out to provide expert commentary on political events. They can most often be found in television studios on election night, at 4am, trying to provide some intelligent remarks as the national results come in. Often the remarks become less intelligent as the night goes on.

They appear on television panels alongside politicians as balance to the partisan representatives – they are the only person on the panel to not claim to have 'won' the election regardless of the results. The proliferation of media channels means that more pundits must be found to fill the space, so opportunities abound for the Professors of Politics at all those former polytechnics with grand-sounding new names, ex-Ministers and political hacks.

The best at it is Peter Snow, who is a master of punditry, and whose swingometers and computer graphics are the stuff of legend. His enthusiasm for the results from Sandwell Borough Council in the small hours is infectious, and it is Snow who often carries an Election Night Special when all around are exhausted and have said all they can say.

Policy wonks

The Policy wonk is the policy expert. These people are perhaps the strangest of the political tribes. The word 'wonk' implies the eccentric nature of the tribe – it sounds almost alien. Wonks are employed by parties and think-tanks to do the thinking that politicians have neither the time nor inclination (or in most cases the aptitude) to do. They are more than simply researchers. Researchers are ten-a-penny. Wonks don't research. They think. They write books and articles about their thoughts. They discuss their thoughts with others of their tribe.

The basic characteristic of the wonk is fearsome and intimidating intelligence. The Tory wonk David Willetts was nick-named 'two-brains' and the size of most wonks' brains is often compared favourably with continents or even stellar bodies. ('Brain the size of Canada', 'Brain the size of a planet', and so on). Most have Firsts from good universities (Oxford, Cambridge, Edinburgh at a pinch), with a second degree from MIT, Harvard or the Sorbonne thrown in. Work abroad is important – a spell with a US Senator or an international management consultancy or bank.

Secondary characteristics tend to be disarming youth, ability to write books, pamphlets, speeches and papers at breakneck speed, and a slight dislocation from everyday life. They may be signed-up party members, but it is rare to see them staffing a street-stall or attending a councillor's surgery. This can lead to a rarified form of discourse and a lack of the common touch. It was a policy wonk, after all, who put the phrase 'post-neo classical endogenous growth theory' into the mouth of the otherwise intelligible Gordon Brown. Because they are not elected, but depend instead on political patronage, they can be sniffy and off-hand to others in a way politicians cannot.

Some cross from wonk to politician. The Tory Party has always been very good at incubating wonks inside the policy unit at Number Ten or in Conservative Central Office, before unleashing them on an unsuspecting constituency. That's where John Redwood came from, and Danny Finkelstein, the Tories' chief wonk is currently seeking the support of the voters of Harrow.

Matthew Taylor is a prominent Labour wonk – he has served as head of policy at party headquarters and now heads up a think-tank, the Institute for Public Policy Research. He claims that in order to dispel any rumours that he was seeking to move from being a wonk to being a candidate, he dyed his hair an Eninem-style blond, which no constituency Labour Party in the country would ever vote for, thus killing the speculation stone-dead.

The ability to read and quote in a foreign language is important to wonks. Many political ideas come from abroad. Countries fall in and out of favour as models to emulate – one minute the Swedish model is hot, next it is New Zealand, or Germany, or the USA. Like policy *conquistadors*, wonks will strip the best ideas from foreign political systems and bring them triumphantly home. So being able to follow the debate in *le Monde* or *Neue Zuricher Zeitung* is vital. Better still is to be able to wade through philosophical texts in the original language. Every wonk should have a well-read copy of the Italian political scientist Norberto Bobbio's seminal work *Left and Right*. But the elders of the tribe have read *Destra e Sinistra* in the original Italian.

The wonk's dream is to invent a new word or concept. New-ness is the policy wonk's currency, and they are driven by the alchemist's fervour to turn base thoughts into political gold. 'Stakeholding.' 'The Third Way.' 'Communitarianism.' 'The Underclass.' 'Social entrepreneurship.' These political buzz-phrases are coined, form the basis of seminars and pamphlets, are torn to pieces, and are superseded by the next concept to come along, all within months. 'Socialism', 'Liberalism', 'Capitalism' – these concepts have lasted for centuries. 'Stakeholding' came and went with the speed of an England football manager. Political ideas are part of our consumer society – there is always a new, better model around the corner, and the old one can be safely thrown away.

The wonk can be found inside the political party structures, as Directors of Research or Heads of Policy. The Conservatives have a long pedigree of wonks, stretching back to the days of Margaret Thatcher's Number Ten Policy Unit and the Conservative Research Department. Others can be found in the world of think-tanks – the Institute for Public Policy Research (IPPR), Demos, the Social Market Foundation (SMF), the Institute for Economic Affairs (IEA), the Adam Smith Institute.

Politics is a battle of ideas as well as organisation, and all political creeds need to be updated and tested against a rapidly changing world. Politicians have no time for reading lengthy political tomes and foreign academic magazines. That is where the wonk comes in, creating new ways to discuss political ideas and making politicians sound well-read.

Journalists

The journalists who follow politics in Parliament are known as 'the Lobby'. The Lobby is a members-only club, with special privileges and its own officials and rules. Being a member of the Lobby is a bit like being a battery hen – kept in isolation, removed from the other hens and force-fed garbage. The difference is that battery hens are worthy of sympathy.

People may have an image of political journalists such as Woodward or Bernstein, ferreting out the truth in the face of government cover-up and official stonewalling. The reality is that ninety per cent of political news journalism is handed on a plate to journalists by either official party sources – the spin doctors – or by maverick rent-a-quotes, or by politicians briefing against one another.

Lobby journalists develop relationships with particular politicians or party officials, and come to rely on regular insights and exclusives. They will often pool information with other Lobby journalists, with whom they work in small, overcrowded offices in the Houses of Parliament. There's a Press Room, where press releases are deposited every day containing news from Government Departments and the Opposition Parties, and there is the Press Gallery, above the Speaker's Chair which overlooks the Chamber of the House of Commons. The Member's Lobby, to the left of the Central Lobby, is reserved for MPs and journalists only, and it is here that facts, news, gossip and rumour are exchanged. There is no shortage of information for the Lobby journalist – their skill comes in deciding what matters and what doesn't, and finding out the story before anyone else.

Political journalists enjoy influence, status, the confidence of powerful figures, and all without having to face the electorate. They can offer their views and conjecture without fear of being voted out of office; they can be as unpopular as you like, and stay in their jobs. Sometimes this power without responsibility can go to their heads. During Labour Party conference 2000 in Brighton, a poster-van paraded up and down the seafront with a giant picture of the *Sun's* political correspondent Trevor Kavanagh bearing the legend 'The most influential man in politics'. Without wishing to cause Mr Kavanagh, whom I do not know, any offence, I can think of at least 150 elected politicians who are higher up the list of influence than him. It was the *Sun*, it will be recalled, which claimed after the 1992 general election that 'it was the Sun wot won it' for John Major. Newspapers with an inflated sense of their own importance are every bit as dangerous as politicians who have lost their sense of perspective.

During an election campaign, political journalists are expelled, as are politicians, from the comfortable surroundings of Westminster. They are sent by their editors around the country to cover the election, on Campaign Buses with candidates, or left in London to cover the election press conferences, where there is even more spoon-feeding. One reason why the coverage of elections can focus on the bizarre and trivial is because it is unscripted and beyond the control of the campaign managers. It gives the journalists a sense of freedom, like dogs let off the leash.

In a world where the media helps determine elections, political journalists have assumed an importance and place at the top table which would make Churchill or Attlee spin in their graves.

3   Planning Your Campaign

Getting selected

> 'He knows nothing; he thinks he knows everything – that clearly points to a career in politics.'
>
> G. B. Shaw

First, as Mrs Beaton might have said, you have to get selected.

The main parties choose their candidates at a local level. For 'safe seats', whoever is selected for the party which holds the seat is almost certain to get elected and stay there as long as they want, which means that the real election is the one that takes place within the party. That means that selection battles can be keenly fought and contested by hundreds of candidates. The Labour Party has a system of local branch nominations, followed by a one-member-one-vote ballot of all party members in a constituency. The party's ruling body, the National Executive Committee, then ratifies the local party's choice. In the lead-up to the 2001 general election, Labour had a 'national panel' of candidates who had been 'pre-approved' by the NEC after a series of interviews and tests. This enabled the party to weed out those prospective candidates who were not suitable.

The Tories have always had a national 'approved list'. To get on the list is a serious business. Candidates to be candidates are interviewed by a panel of three officials, and then by one of the party's Deputy Chairmen. Once approved by them, the candidate is sent on a weekend 'parliamentary selection board'. If they pass that, their names are added to the national list. Then a local constituency must select them. The local Conservative Associations have a Candidate Selection Committee which sifts through CVs and then the local Executive interviews candidates (and sometimes their spouses). They then draw up a final shortlist. Those that have survived thus far are invited to a members' general meeting to make a speech and take questions, and the members present vote for their choice.

The Liberal Democrats have a very simple system of one member one vote, so the candidate with the most votes from local members wins. They have a national list of approved candidates, and the selections are overseen by the Joint States Candidates Committee. Local parties' executives draw up the shortlist, which must include at least one man and one woman.

Smaller parties, such as the Greens, simply ask for volunteers and try to stand as many candidates as they can.

If you don't fancy any of the mainstream parties, you can always found your own party and make sure you are selected. Oswald Mosley (the New Party), Arthur Scargill (Socialist Labour Party), the Gang of Four (Social Democratic Party), and James Goldsmith (Referendum Party) all tried it, with roughly the same levels of success.

Or you can stand as an independent, as 'a laugh', to draw attention to a particular issue, or to plug a commercial interest. Martin Bell stood as an anti-sleaze independent candidate in Tatton in 1997 and in Brentwood and Ongar at the 2001 general election. Bell is the first independent (ie non-party) MP to be elected for fifty years. The following independents have stood for by-elections since 1992:

Conservative Party Rebel
People and Pensioners Party
21st Century Party
Give the Royal Billions to Schools
Sack Graham Taylor
Buy the Daily Sport
Highlander IV Wednesday Promotion Night
House Homeless People
Forest – Freedom of Choice for Smokers
Free Para Lee Clegg Now
Mark Thomas Friday Nights Channel Four
Official News Bunny
Stop Conservatives Poncing on Tobacco Companies
Daily and Sunday Sport
Reform 2000 Anti-VAT
Legalise Cannabis Alliance
Wales on Sunday Match Funding Now

Campaign for Living Will Legislation
Equal Parenting Party
Status Quo
Hamilton Accies Home Watson Away

There have also been candidates who have stood in a deliberate attempt to confuse the voters. Candidates have stood as 'Literal Democrat' 'Conversative' or 'New Labour'. Sometimes people change their names and stand with the same, or similar, name as the MP. Alice Mahon MP faced a male opponent in 1997 – called Alice Mahon. The Registration of Political Parties Act is designed to prevent people standing under deliberately confusing party names, and allows party logos to appear on the ballot paper for the first time.

Back in the mainstream parties, being local is seen as a huge help in getting selected. During selection battles, putative candidates will discover long-lost relatives in the constituency, recall fondly great-grandparents who owned the local butchers or ran the local pub, and refer mournfully to their ancestors buried in the local cemetery.

In elections, voters can be resentful of 'carpet-baggers' looking to be elected, as Roy Jenkins found out during the Hillhead by-election in 1982. On meeting a man of Asian origin Jenkins asked 'How long have you been here?' to which the man replied 'a lot longer than you.'

Some candidates really are local, of course. Being leader of the local council or owner of the local factory can have obvious advantages. Many Labour candidates for Parliament are local councillors first, and can build their alliances and support within the local Labour Party – one reason why there are so many former council leaders in the Parliamentary Labour Party. David Blunkett, Graham Stringer, Ian Coleman, Tony Coleman and Frank Dobson are former council leaders, to name but a few. David Lammy, the new MP for Tottenham, and the youngest MP in the House, made much of his local credentials during selection in 2000. His Tottenham background probably counted for as much as his Harvard degree and brilliant career as a lawyer.

But other candidates are selected without any local credentials. - Hilary Benn won the Labour nomination in Leeds Central in 1999 without any obvious history in the city, and Dominic Grieve won the Tories' nomination in Beaconsfield in 1997 without any link to the constituency at all. Grieve even told his selection meeting that he would not be relocating his family from London if he won.

Just as local parties can select candidates, they can also deselect them. If they think you're not doing a good job, or you take up a position on an issue with which they violently disagree, local activists may get rid of you.

Developments in campaigning

In Britain, general election campaigns last between three and six weeks, with Polling Day on a Thursday of the Prime Minister's choosing. The traditional image of an election is local activists knocking on doors and giving out leaflets and candidates driving around in loudspeaker vans. The campaign was a collection of 600-odd local constituency contests, with local people choosing their local MP, and the government being formed by whichever party won the most seats.

It is debatable how far this traditional image was ever accurate. Certainly in the twentieth century many elections were decided on national rather than local issues, such as the election of the National Government in 1931 or the Labour Government in 1945. The Presidential style of campaigning, with the focus on the party leader such as Churchill, has been around for decades. But through the 1980s and 1990s, the traditional election campaign was killed off by the importation and deployment of a range of campaigning techniques, some borrowed from advertising and marketing, some borrowed from elections abroad, notably in the USA, and some developed at home.

The main developments since 1945 have been:
• the professionalisation of electioneering
• the centralisation of campaigns
• the increased length of campaigns.

The professionalisation of campaigns

Election campaigns are based on the need to win votes, and so they owe their origins to the extension of the democratic franchise in the nineteenth century, and the extension of votes to women in the twentieth century. In the early days, candidates would seek to reach as many voters as possible in person. In the US, candidates would speak from the back of trains, stopping every station, over thousands of miles of track. William Gladstone's Midlothian campaign in 1879–80 was a herculean effort to speak to as many voters in public meetings as possible. During the 1924 general election, Ramsay MacDonald gave speeches in 16 constituencies in a single day.

The need to reach voters has driven the search for ever more efficient ways to find, persuade, and catalogue them. As technology advanced, so campaigning techniques advanced. The telephone is a more efficient way of reaching people than knocking on doors. Radio is better than public meetings. Television is better than radio. Email is better than television. Direct mail is better than leaflets. The emergence of mass communications led to the emergence of mass campaigning – and *de facto*, to a new breed of media-savvy politician. There are a host of great politicians who would not have survived in the modern media age. You cannot imagine the mild-mannered and taciturn Attlee or the frequently-drunk Asquith appearing on a chat-show. Stanley Baldwin and Franklin D. Roosevelt used radio broadcasts to great effect in the thirties. In the forties, Churchill used radio to give his most inspiring and famous speeches. Baldwin's fame did not extend universally, however. On a train a fellow passenger tapped the Prime Minister on the knee. 'You're Baldwin, aren't you? You were at Harrow in '84' said the man. 'Yes, that's right' said Baldwin. After a pause, the man said: 'Tell me, what are you doing now?'

The arrival of television as a form of mass communication did most to move electioneering from an amateur to a professional activity. A new breed of campaign professionals emerged within the party structures – men and women with expertise in journalism and broadcasting, political projection, and local election techniques. Outside the traditional political structures, experts from the world of advertising, marketing, opinion polling, and public relations came forward to offer their services to the political parties. The Conservatives, with their overlap with the world of business, were always more receptive to the offers of help from professional communicators.

Labour politicians historically felt there was something distasteful about using the same techniques to sell soap as to sell socialism. Some believed that advertising was a fundamentally corrupt practice which would corrupt politics if allowed any influence. Books like *The Hidden Persuaders* in the 1950s, which revealed the underhand psychological tricks that advertisers played, stoked the paranoia. So professional political communications techniques were, until the mid-eighties, the preserve of the Conservative Party. Margaret Thatcher's slick use of poster advertising, media management, photo-opportunities and personal presentation stood in sharp contrast to Labour's shambolic and out-of-touch approach to the electorate. In the 1983 general election, hundreds of Labour supporters would flock to hear Michael Foot at inspiring rallies all over the country, while the Tories were reaching millions of key swing voters in marginal seats via the television, radio and tabloid newspapers.

The arrival of Peter Mandelson as Labour's Director of Communications in 1985 marked the turning-point in the professionalisation of Labour's communications. The creation of the Shadow Communications Agency, drawing on the talents of Labour supporters in advertising, PR and polling meant that Labour could match the Tories' expertise. The Labour Party won the 1987 campaign hands-down – their campaign was professional, on-message, lively and dynamic. The Hugh Hudson-directed 'Kinnock, the Movie' party election broadcast stands as a masterpiece of political communications. But Labour lost, because its policies, especially on defence, were unpopular.

Following Bill Clinton's victory in 1992, Labour strategists forged close links with the Democrat campaigners and learned the lessons of Clinton's success. The need for a centralised election 'War Room' (a phrase coined, in the context of elections, by Hillary Clinton) backed by a large team of researchers to direct the campaign centrally, the use of vigorous 'rapid rebuttal' of the Republicans' claims, flexibility of tactics, and lightning reactions summed up in the phrase 'Speed Kills' were all features of Clinton's Little Rock campaign which were borrowed wholesale by Labour. Senior Labour figures such as Alan Barnard, John Braggins and Margaret McDonagh visited the USA in 1992 and reported back to Labour on the ground-breaking election techniques.

Labour's Millbank operation between 1995 and 1997 stands as the most professional campaign structure ever created by a British political party. Compared to the campaigns fought from Labour's Walworth Road headquarters, or Transport House before that, Millbank was a world apart. During the 1992 campaign, when I worked at Walworth Road, the campaign was divided all over the place. The 'anchor researchers' covering specific policy areas were in the basement, which had been used to store old posters until the day before the campaign. The 'Economic Secretariat' – the economy, tax, and business specialists under John Smith – were in a different building next door. There were conflicting instructions coming from the Leader's Office and the Shadow Communications Agency. When Labour's campaign took hits such as over Jennifer's Ear, the election broadcast about the unfairness of private medical treatment, they caused panic and turmoil at the heart of the campaign and blew the campaign off-course for days.

Millbank in 1997 was the antithesis of that. By creating an operation on a single open-plan floor, the lines of communication were open and flowed from the centre. There were clear lines of command and control. People had defined roles and knew what they were doing. There were clear political messages and themes, and a well-worked out campaign. It could be argued that Labour was always going to win the 1997 general election, but the emphatic swing and the size of the majority must owe a great deal to the professional campaign.

Political campaigning in Britain will continue to professionalise. What American politics does today often ends up being done tomorrow in Britain. It is easy to over-estimate the 'Americanisation' of British politics - the structure and culture of British politics mitigates against wholesale emulation of the American system. But features of American politics, especially the use of the Internet as a campaign, fundraising, and political education tool, and the rise of the 'campaign consultant' for hire to the highest bidder, will take hold in Britain within a few years.

The centralisation of campaigns

No national political party leaves their local campaigns to chance. Once, the local party members would select their candidate, raise some funds to pay for the deposit, newsletters and posters, and set off round the constituency with soapbox, posters and wallpaper paste and try to win votes. Each constituency would have its own local electoral addresses and campaign issues. The role of the national party leaders was to make speeches at public meetings and rallies, and to fight their own constituency campaign. Today, the local party candidate is part of a national campaign, and the local campaign is a subsidiary part of a centrally-choreographed national campaign.

For example, as Margaret McDonagh has said of the 1997 campaign 'ultimately, the party member knocking on the door would be saying the same thing as Tony Blair on *News at Ten*.' Campaigns have become centralised. Party headquarters see local candidates and activists as their local representatives, there to do the central campaign planners' bidding and work to a national plan.

Local campaigns are controlled through the strict timetabling of campaign themes and visits by key campaigners, the mass production of campaign materials for local distribution, the dissemination of campaign messages, often with a local twist, via email or fax, and strict controls on political activity.

But this centralisation of themes, materials and messages does not mean the death of the local campaign. Indeed, the greater support that national party offices can give local campaigns means that local campaigns can be lively, professional and match what is going on in the national media. In local elections, there is less centralisation because of the very nature of a local election – it is about the local town hall and local services, so the issues tend to be more local. This gives a greater opportunity for a candidate to organise a professional and effective campaign addressing national and local issues.

The level of logistical support means that campaigning materials can be high-quality and eye-catching. The flow of policy information, particularly via email, means that the candidate can be fully informed about political developments and arguments. The co-ordination of media messages means that the candidate always has material for the local newspapers and radio programmes. Centralisation means that the modern candidate can enjoy a higher level of support and guidance than at any previous election.

The increased length of campaigns

Campaigns today last months and years, not days and weeks. The timeframe for campaigns is being stretched. In Britain, the timing of election campaigns is determined by the electoral cycle and the decision of the Prime Minister to 'go to the country', so there is not a defined pre-election period, but the UK is seeing a move to the American feature of 'long' and 'permanent' campaigns. The long campaign might be seen as the twelve months before an election, when politics is dominated by battles for electoral advantage and point-scoring. During this period, the usual business of government and Opposition, including policy announcements, reshuffles of Cabinets, and Budgets, is skewed by the considerations of the impending election.

At the local level, once candidates have been selected, campaign activity is stepped up and intensified for this strategically important period. From the end of the party conference season in 2000 to polling day in the 2001 general election, Britain was experiencing the 'long campaign'.

The logic of this elongation of the time spent campaigning is the shift to the 'permanent campaign', which means politics is perpetually conducted at the same pace and frenetic level of activity as the middle of an election campaign. For example, it has been estimated that Ronald Reagan, a successful electioneer, dedicated two-thirds of his time as President on public duties in the full glare of the media, and only one-third on policy and governance.

The American political strategist Dick Morris argues that the permanent campaign means that politicians need to maintain a permanent majority. The elected politician's 'functional strength ebbs and flows with his popularity as it is measured in weekly tracking polls throughout his term ... when he dips below fifty per cent, he is functionally out of office.' Morris's conclusion is that 'each day is election day in modern America'. This explains a great deal about American politics, but it is also terrible advice for British politicians. Those with a mandate have to be right as well as popular, and the point of a five-year term of office is to allow governments to govern over an electoral and economic cycle. Governments' popularity tends to dip mid-term ('the mid-term blues') and recover as the election approaches.

Often governments take unpopular short-term decisions in order for medium-term advantage. Chancellor Gordon Brown's adherence to the Tory spending targets for the first two years in office 1997-99 was attacked for its frugality at the time, but allowed economic stability, debt reduction, and increased investment in the latter stages of the government. Between her election in 1979 and the Falklands War, Margaret Thatcher sent shockwaves through the economy and was the most unpopular Prime Minister ever, yet she went on to win two more elections. If all politicians were concerned about was their popularity, nothing would ever get done.

Labour started its period in office from 1997 as though the election was still going on. The party spin doctors were moved into Government Departments as Special Advisers, and the hyperbole of electioneering persisted into the more sedate pattern of official government announcements. Peter Mandelson recalls: 'The enthusiasm of our rhetoric did not help ... we were all a bit guilty of letting some of our sense of the possible get out of sync with the pace of change on the ground.'

So while the popular mood must be a constant factor on politicians' decisions, backed by expert polling and research, a responsible politician will act in ways which will not be immediately popular, for the good of the country in the longer term. Every day is not election day – only election day is election day. In office, every day is the day you fulfil your promises to the people who put you there.

Drawing up your plan

For your campaign to take shape and organisation, at a local, regional, or national level, you must have a plan. It could be a single side of A4, or a thick wad of papers. Without it, your election campaign will lack focus, squander resources, burn out your activists and volunteers, and suffer from what the military call 'mission drift'. You will also find yourself buffeted by your opponents and always reacting to their agenda and on the back foot. Political parties employ teams to plan national election campaigns for years ahead of polling day. Their deliberations are collated into a 'war book', which contains all the elements of the campaign, including the key messages, the strengths and weaknesses of the election protagonists, the methods of delivery, and the timetable for media events and campaign visits. During the 1997 general election, an early version of the Labour war book found its way into the hands of the Conservatives, who gleefully handed out copies to the media, and indeed passers-by outside Conservative Central Office. The document shows the level of both strategic thinking and tactical detail which goes into a campaign plan, and also the frank nature of the assessments of strengths and weaknesses.

At the constituency level, the campaign plan forms part of a larger national plan. A local campaign plan helps target your resources, ensures that all your volunteers are pulling in the same direction, gives a shared understanding of what you are attempting to achieve, and gives you a compass by which to steer your activities. Advance planning and preparation can save valuable time and money as the campaign develops.

Campaigns are drawn up onto a 'grid'. What is the grid? In modern political campaigning, the grid has assumed the role of Bible, Koran, Torah and any other sacred text you can name. It is guarded with the secrecy of *Enigma*, and like the holy books of Mediaeval times, can only be viewed by the chosen few. In essence, the grid is the nuts and bolts of the party's campaign plan, distilled from a thousand meetings and discussions, from the wisdom of pollsters, advisers, strategists and politicians, and forms the strategy that a party will follow during a campaign. Labour's election strategist Philip Gould calls the grid 'the heart of the campaign, bringing together all elements of strategy on one sheet of paper. Without a grid, the campaign cannot really be said to exist.'

At the local level, the campaign grid is simply a timetable of events and targets set out over time, with responsibilities allocated to relevant members of the campaign team.

Your plan should be flexible, and allow for unforeseen developments and opportunities. The best campaigns are those which can quickly react to events and turn the unexpected to their advantage. Your strategy should be soundly worked out, but your tactics should be flexible and adaptable. This adaptability allows you to benefit from your opponents' mistakes, and to maximise your advantages. It allows your campaign to generate momentum – the 'big mo' – as polling day draws near.

The elements of your campaign plan should include:

- Overall strategic objective
- Tactical targets
- Your key messages
- Target audiences
- Methods of delivery
- Timing
- Evaluation of success.

In other words,

- what you want to achieve,
- what are the steps along the way to achieving it
- what you want to say
- who you want to say it to
- how you want to say it
- when and for how long you want to say it
- and how you know if you've been successful.

These are component parts of an election campaign, and you need to be clear what the relevance each of them has to your own campaign. Let us look at each part in some detail.

What do you want to achieve?

You need an objective. Nationally, the parties set themselves campaign objectives. At the 2001 general election, for example, the parties' objectives could be described as:

Labour: to hold every seat (146 of them) it gained in 1997 and stay in office.
Tories: to win enough seats to claim recovery and win next time.
Liberal Democrats: to win every seat they won in 1997 and retain their influence.
Nationalists: to take seats off Labour in the heartlands.

For example, Labour's election campaign strategy for 2001 is called 'Operation Turnout'. It is based on the realisation that whilst in 1997 voters were motivated to come out and vote, in 2001 there could be higher levels of indifference. The challenge is therefore to motivate voters to vote.

You need to decide your own local objectives. Ultimately, you may want to achieve high office, power, world domination or whatever your ambition dictates. But for each election you fight, you need a clear strategic objective. In winner-takes-all politics, the objective may seem obvious: to vanquish your opponents and win the election. But the reality is that this ultimate goal may be electorally impossible, although of course no candidate will ever admit defeat before the results. If you find yourself battling against a politician with a huge majority, you may fight the election as though you mean to win, but have an objective which is more in tune with reality.

If victory seems elusive, you may want your party to come from third place to second place. You may want to see your party's share of the vote increase, or see the actual number of votes increase. You may want to ensure that the sitting politician loses his or her seat, even if it is not you who wins. You may want to increase the number of new party members in a constituency.

These objectives can be discussed with your campaign team and agent, and shared with your campaign volunteers. There might also be some private objectives which you decide upon. These might be about furthering your own political career by being seen to do a good job as a candidate, and place yourself in a position to get a winnable seat next time, or for incumbents, impressing the party leader so that front-bench responsibilities might ensue.

What are the steps along the way to achieving it?

Your strategic aims have been decided – but what are the tactical steps along the way to achieving it? These tactical steps are what give your campaign a trajectory and sense of dynamism. They create milestones along the journey which allow reflection and assessment of success and failure.

For example, the strategic objective of Labour's 'Operation Turnout' has been described, but the tactical targets are:

Phase one
- achieve a contact rate of 50 per cent of the electorate being identified and segmented
- identify all first-time voters
- identify all general election-only voters
- identify low turnout areas

Phase two
- telephone all first-time voters
- blitz all low turnout areas twice
- write to all general election-only voters
- undertake a comprehensive candidate projection programme

Phase Three
- by May 2001, to have developed a relationship with each voter so Labour can influence voting behaviour

Phase Four
- to continue the dialogue with supporters and move them from being weak to strong supporters and to full membership.

Your local campaign might include this kind of activity. You can set all kinds of targets, for example:

- to knock on a door in every street in the constituency
- to raise £2000 for campaign funds by polling day
- to recruit 50 new party members
- to distribute 5000 leaflets every month
- get to 50 per cent contact rate after six months
- blitz one ward every month
- to get at least one story in the local paper every fortnight.

Your targets, whatever you decide they should be, give you something to work towards and can inspire your volunteers to greater efforts. To do this they must be realistic and achievable.

What do you want to say?

You must decide which parts of your political platform you want to concentrate on. You cannot campaign on every issue you may have a view on – you must prioritise. Choosing your issues will depend on the national and local context, and be based on an assessment of areas where you think you are strong compared to areas where your opposition is weak (and they will be doing the same).

The Conservatives may choose areas like taxation, the countryside, asylum seekers, or defence as their strengths.

Labour may choose employment, education, health and pensions.

The Liberal Democrats may campaign on Europe, electoral reform or the environment.

Once you've decided on your battleground issues, you have to hone your messages. These must be distilled into the core messages which will appear on posters, leaflets, election addresses, and on the lips of candidates and campaigners on the doorsteps. As we will see, messages must be crafted into soundbites for the media and for campaign materials, speeches, and conversation with the voters. Campaigns can be fought over very narrow territory, with a range of important issues marginalized or ignored. Often elections are marked by the 'dogs that didn't bark.' In 1992, despite the rise of environmental awareness after the success of the Green Party in the 1989 European elections, the environment hardly featured. Labour's campaign press conference on the environment was cancelled in the wake of the Jennifer's Ear fiasco. The issue, despite its obvious saliency, failed to make any impact on an election campaign which focussed on tax.

Who do you want to say it to?

Targeting is the key concept in all forms of communications including election campaigns. Even with unlimited resources you cannot reach every voter. Within the limited resources of a campaign, you must decide whom you want to reach. The Liberal Democrats pioneered targeting – concentrating their resources on small areas and working them over the years, until council seats multiplied and the work paid off in parliamentary seats. Lib Dems, once elected, are quite hard to get rid of. Logic dictates that you want to reach the people most likely to vote for you – either those who have voted for you before, or those who are considering voting for you: your 'strong vote' and your 'weak vote'. If you are seeking to unseat an incumbent, you need to persuade voters to switch their support from him to you. 'Switchers' can decide an election.

Don't forget that there will be a group of voters who have never voted before – usually those who have turned 18 since the last election. If you can get a first-time voter to support you, you may have a supporter for life.

Targeting can go beyond simple categories of voting behaviour. You can target people because of where they live. If they live in 'marginal' areas where votes are distributed evenly between candidates, they might be able to tip the result in your direction. In a general election, parties focus on the marginal seats which will determine the outcome, and on the wards within those seats where the battle is most keenly fought. These voters' votes count for more than those in 'safe' seats, and their support will be assiduously courted.

As well as communities of geography, there are communities of interest. These communities can be targeted with key messages which appeal to their particular interests. They might include teachers, nurses or trade union members, or animal lovers, or women, or members of a particular ethnic or faith group.

The lesson from commercial marketing is that if you can treat your audience as a series of individuals, with their own concerns and interests, they will be far more receptive to what you have to say. Successful marketing, and successful electoral politics, depends on building a relationship with people, treating them as individuals not as part of some amorphous mass, and dealing with them with respect and courtesy over a sustained period of time. No-one likes being addressed as though part of an anonymous crowd.

This requires excellent data storage and retrieval capability on your part. Every piece of data captured by your canvassing and contact with the electorate must be rigorously recorded and available for use in the future. In the past, this might have involved card indexes and paper files – now it can all be stored on computer.

I heard of one politician who used to scour the local papers every week for the names of local people, either in the news pages, or in the births, marriages and deaths columns, and he would write an appropriate personal letter to them. Over the decades, he built relationships with his local electorate a few at a time. With computer databases, this kind of information can be stored and tracked over the years. He never lost an election.

How do you want to say it?

You can spend every waking hour talking to the voters, and only scratch the surface of a constituency. You must decide what other channels of communication you want to use. These include the local and national media, posters, advertising, leaflets, speeches and meetings, newsletters, and personal contact. All these methods are discussed in detail later on in the book. A good politician will try to spread him or herself as thinly as possible in a constituency, visiting as many places as possible. They will never always drink in the same pub, shop in the same shops, or attend the same church.

I'm told some politicians always use a different taxi company in their constituency, so that as many cabbies as possible can say to their passengers 'I had that MP in the back of my cab last week.' Edinburgh MP Nigel Griffiths pioneered the 'Nigel calling' method of contacting voters. His team would put cards though voters' doors saying that Nigel would be in the street next week. If they wanted to meet him, all they had to do was leave the card in the window, and Nigel would knock on their door. That way, Nigel Griffiths could meet many more of his constituents than he would through old-fashioned canvassing.

NIGEL GRIFFITHS MP

CALLING

NEXT

FRIDAY

MORNING

LABOUR MEMBER OF PARLIAMENT FOR SOUTH EDINBURGH

Dear Resident,

I am calling on local residents next Friday between 10.15am and 1pm. If you would like to meet me to discuss any issues or problems, please phone 662 4520 and I'll arrange to see you.

However, if Friday is not convenient and you would like me to call at another time, just ring 662 4520 and I'll find a day and time to suit you. Alternatively, you may prefer to write to me at 31 Minto Street, Edinburgh, EH9 2BN.

Yours sincerely,

Nigel Griffiths

HERE TO HELP   www.griffithsmp.co.uk

When and for how long do you want to say it?

'When?' is an important question. You must reserve some energy for the short campaign – the month before polling day. But if you leave all your campaign until then, it may be too late. You must pace your campaign over the months, with different phases of activity and benchmarks and targets along the way. There's no point knocking on doors during the day as most people will be at work. In the evenings, though, people might not come to their doors after dark. Campaigning in the high street or shopping centre is best left until Saturdays, when people are out and about. So you must work out the optimum times to reach your target voters and make the best use of your volunteers' time.

You can use certain points in the calendar as pegs for campaigning. On Mothers Day, Valentine's Day, and the lead-up to Christmas, for example, you can run campaigning activities with a theme – what you'll do for mothers, what policies you want for Christmas and so on. When the clocks went back in Autumn 2000, Labour campaigners across the country gave out leaflets with 'Don't let the Tories turn the clocks back' and even projected William Hague's face onto Big Ben.

You should create a big splash as soon as the election is called, so that voters see you at the railway station or in the street on the day the media is announcing the election. Towards the end of the campaign you need to create a sense of momentum – try getting a new, different poster put up in your supporters' windows, make the size and shape of your newsletters or leaflets bigger, step up the last minute knocking on doors. In the last week of 1997, all Labour's materials turned purple, so that everything felt fresh and exciting.

How you know if you've been successful?

This last one may sound strange – surely the way to know whether you've been successful is whether your side won or not. However, whilst no candidate ever sets out to lose, in some circumstances where victory would require a political earthquake, increasing the share of the vote, increasing the number of votes, or coming second instead of third, might be seen as notable achievements in their own right.

As we have seen, there will be tactical targets as the campaign develops. If you hit them, use the small successes as an excuse to take your volunteers for a drink and say thanks. If you miss them, sit down and work out why, and adjust future targets accordingly.

Assembling your campaign team

Your campaign will depend on the efforts of volunteer activists who are motivated by your cause and want to see you win. At the local level, few parties can afford professional staff. In Britain, the parties are like standing armies of volunteers, active all year round. In the USA, campaigners are like territorial reserves, who come together for single campaigns or around particular candidates.

The success of your campaign will depend on the quality and enthusiasm of your volunteer helpers. But because volunteers are not paid and are not part of formal party structures, they cannot be treated like employees. Their motivations and expectations are different, and the pitfalls are greater.

You may want to appoint a Volunteer Manager, so that the day-to-day allocation of tasks is conducted effectively, and the candidate is not seen to be ordering people around.

Other jobs which need allocating are:

Campaign Manager – the person with the ultimate authority on all matters relating to the campaign. This should not be the candidate, who has other things to do.

Agent – a legal position with an enormous amount of responsibility. It is Agents who can go to jail if election law is broken. This should be a trusted and experienced figure.

IT manager – someone to co-ordinate all your IT, set-up the campaign computers and printers, manage databases, and fix problems. You may also want a *Web Manager* to look after your cyber-campaign.

Press Officer – to deal with all aspects of your media relations activity including setting up photo-opportunities, answering press enquiries, drafting news releases and organising letter-writing.

Volunteer workers can range from those with a couple of hours spare a month to those such as unemployed or part-time workers, or retired people, who can volunteer full-time. Some of your helpers may be experienced campaigners, former agents, candidates or MPs, and their experience and knowledge should be welcomed.

Some volunteers will emerge organically as the result of high-profile campaigning activity. The harder you campaign, the more volunteers you attract. All political activists, even the most hardened, started somewhere. They will come with a range of skills and experience, from enthusiastic 'envelope stuffers' to top fundraisers, journalists or celebrities. You may want to 'vet' new volunteers to ensure they are not infiltrators from your opponent's camp.

You should conduct a 'skills audit' of your volunteers – do they have particular skills such as IT, design, copy-writing, or accounting – and take full details including their addresses, emails, phone numbers and next-of-kin details for all your volunteers.

Do your volunteers have access to resources such as premises, cars, photocopiers, computers or services-in-kind which can be utilised for the campaign? Are your volunteers part of other networks such as community groups or trade unions which your campaign can plug into? Make the most of existing networks.

You must ensure that volunteers are performing appropriate tasks – don't send the oldest pensioner off to leaflet the biggest housing estate, and make sure that no-one is sent out knocking on doors on their own or after dark.

You have to be tough sometimes – you are running a serious campaign not a drop-in centre. If volunteers are creating more problems than they are solving, or are behaving inappropriately with other people, or misrepresenting your campaign, they should be asked to leave the campaign.

If you can, offer training in the activities of your campaign such as computer databasing, or writing news releases, or preparing leaflets so that volunteers feel they are learning from their time with the campaign, and have skills to share next time. Have regular volunteer meetings so that everyone has a shared understanding of goals and what needs to be done to achieve them. Ask people for ideas and views on the conduct of the campaign. Listen to what they say. Make people feel part of something important – offer certificates for volunteers, or special tee-shirts, or a special team photograph or a roll of honour.

On election day, make sure refreshments are available, and as candidate, make a point of making the tea for the volunteers. I saw John Prescott take a tray of tea and biscuits to a room full of campaigners during a by-election, and I bet they've never forgotten it. And always say *thank you*.

Campaign headquarters

Your campaign needs an HQ. This might be someone's house or a disused shop or offices, hired for the duration of the campaign. If you can choose the ideal location, go for a shop with a front on the main shopping area or thoroughfare so your HQ becomes part of the marketing of the campaign. Use the shop window for posters, displays and the campaign phone numbers. You can decorate the walls with newspaper clippings and photographs about the campaign, faxes from your party leader thanking your volunteers, and charts showing your targets and how near you are to achieving them.

You should keep the place as tidy as possible, and ban smoking. For parliamentary elections, each ward can be allocated its own large plastic tray so that leaflets can be distributed to their deliverers and canvass returns submitted without anything getting lost under mounds of paper and rubbish.

There should be a ready supply of tea and biscuits, toilet facilities, and a quiet room for the candidate to recover his or her composure.

After the campaign is over, leave the place tidy, and remember to take down the external posters and hoardings, especially if you lost the election. You don't want your faded old posters becoming covered in graffiti. If you win, you may want to convert the campaign HQ into a constituency office.

Fundraising

While British politics is not lubricated with the phenomenal amounts of cash that splash around the American body-politic, you do need some money to run a campaign. Local political parties should focus on fundraising all year round as a way of maintaining their links with their members and in order to build up a 'war chest' ready for the election. You should have monthly or quarterly targets as part of your campaign plan.

Some fundraising can be part of a social programme. Few party supporters resent being asked to a dinner, with a raffle or auction, which has a strong fundraising element. If people are enjoying themselves, seeing old friends and meeting new ones, they will happily part with their cash. They will also be more likely to want to take part in political campaigning once they have met like-minded people in a convivial setting.

It is an obvious facet of human nature that we want something back for our money, so if fundraising can be tied into some kind of benefits for the donor it is more likely to meet with success, as long as the benefits are a warm feeling inside rather than preferential treatment for planning permission.

Other fundraising can be more overt, especially as the election nears.

Types of fundraising include:

Direct appeals, via telephone or letter

A direct approach to a large number of people via a letter or telephone calls can raise funds by the fiver or tenner, but this method requires a lot of effort for a low level of return. If people give a tenner, they may feel they have done their bit and be immunised to further appeals. It is better to get donors to sign up to a standing order or direct debit so that amounts are regularly received. A single donation can outstrip the effort of raising money by small degrees.

A personal approach by a 'peer'

Wealthy people are more likely to donate larger sums of money, in the hundreds and thousands, if approached by a 'peer' – someone in the same income bracket that they respect. These can only be done on a one-on-one basis and conducted with great tact and diplomacy. You must be sure that the individual shares your enthusiasm for your cause, and is likely to want to contribute to campaign funds. Personal giving of large sums can only be conducted in an ethical framework and a clear understanding that campaign contributions do not confer special privileges if the favoured candidate is elected.

Dinners and drinks

Anything with a strong social element is an excellent way of raising funds while fulfilling other important tasks like energising your supporters and encouraging new people. If you have a supporter with a large house who is willing to support an event, you can ask others to bring food and drink for a fundraising supper or coffee morning. Some people will happily make a cake or buy a crate of beer who would never consider going out canvassing. People can pay a sum for their ticket, and you raise funds while having a good time. You might be lucky enough to find a local restaurant or curry house willing to host a special buffet for Sunday lunch as a special fundraiser.

Raffles

Raffles can be regularly conducted before campaign and party meetings, with small prizes such as a box of chocolates or bottle of wine. If you manage to raise a few pounds each week, it will soon mount up.

Auctions

Auctions can raise funds as part of a fun night out. The trick is to have all the lots for auction donated, so that all takings are profit. Lots might include signed copies of politicians' books, bottles of House of Commons whisky and boxes of mints, meals for two in local restaurants, or tea on the Terrace of the Commons. You can also try to get one-off and novelty items which cannot be bought in a shop, such as one of Tony Blair's ties or William Hague's baseball cap. You should appoint a good auctioneer for the evening – someone who will give the event a sense of occasion and entice people into making bids.

Bingo or scratch cards

Gambling can be used to raise funds. Some local political parties run their own scratch card promotions which volunteers take round door-to-door to sell to known customers. I used to sell these scratch cards on a housing estate in Hammersmith for the London Labour Party, and it seemed to me unethical to sell five pounds worth of scratch cards every week to people who were plainly out of work or on low wages, but with the money raised, the Labour Party employed full-time agents and helped win the election. You could argue that the money was put to good use, unlike the profits amassed by Camelot.

You might organise bingo evenings or 'race nights' where people can bet on horse racing shown on a video screen, or even casino nights with roulette wheels, where the house takings are put straight into campaign coffers.

Elections cost money, even just for the deposit, and unless you are an eccentric millionaire it is better to raise small amounts from lots of people to finance your campaign rather than be in hock to a small number of wealthy people.

What is your policy?

This book is not about policy (there are already plenty of those), but every candidate needs to be clear what their policies are. The policies you stand for – the things you want to do with the power you seek – are at the heart of your campaign. The policies you believe in are distilled into your campaign messages and soundbites, they are the subject of your speeches, leaflets and manifesto, they are the answers on the doorsteps to the voters' concerns, and importantly they are your guide to action if elected. So you'd better have some, and know what they are.

The role of the candidate in an election campaign is not to devise policy. That should have been done for you beforehand. Political parties make policy through various and convoluted means. They use their internal policy departments and wonks, and can call on affiliated think-tanks. Party members can have a role. Labour and Liberal Democrats have policy-making conferences which debate and decide policy priorities. Labour has a mammoth system of policy forums, commissions and conferences which set out the policies that form the bedrock of the manifesto.

You should spend time working out your line on a range of issues, both local and national, because you can be sure to be asked at some point in the campaign. The issues you can be confident that will come up include:

Abortion
Age of Consent for gays
AIDS
Air Traffic Control (privatisation of)
Animal welfare
Animal experiments
Asylum Seekers
Benefits
Bosnia
Business rates
Cannabis (legalisation of)
Child Support Agency
Crime
Cyprus
Councils
Countryside
Death Penalty
Defence
Disability rights
The Dome
England's football manager
Education
Electoral reform

Europe
Euthanasia
Health
Far East POWs
Farming
Flood defences
Fox Hunting
Grammar Schools
Immigration
Israel/Palestine
Noisy neighbours
Northern Ireland
Nuclear weapons
Monarchy
Pensions
Petrol prices
Section 28
Smoking
Race relations
Tax
Third World Debt
Transport, especially public transport
Unions
University tuition fees

By the time the election comes around, the policy platforms have been worked out and tested. The candidate's job is to learn the policies, be confident in explaining and defending them, and to hide any personal differences with the official view. In this regard, the political parties have centralised control over local campaigns, but it does mean that local MPs, if elected, are bound by the same manifesto and voters know, more or less, what to expect. When candidates go it alone, as when Conservative candidates start ruling out the single currency in their election addresses irrespective of the national party line, the media have a field day. Such independence of thought is seen as evidence of splits and dissent in the ranks, and that makes a good story for journalists.

Journalists and your opponents may try to catch you out over other issues which are closer to home. You must be sure you know:

- the price of a pint of milk
- the price of a litre of petrol
- the price of a loaf of bread
- the local football team's latest result
- price of a local bus ticket.

When, in 1995, Kenneth Clarke as Chancellor of the Exchequer appeared on BBC Radio Newcastle he wanted to appear as though he had local knowledge so he praised the local steelworks. Unfortunately, it had closed down in 1981. Two weeks later he praised the local nappy manufacturing. The nappy factory had closed in 1991. Whoever was briefing him was doing a shockingly bad job.

You might even consider getting a crash course in what's going on in the TV soaps, what acts are in the charts, who the hot actors and actresses are, what must-have toy every child wants for Christmas and what people are watching on television. On a visit to the set of *Coronation Street*, Tony Blair was briefed about the programme by a party staffer, as the PM never had time to watch it. As he toured round the Granada studios with actress Liz Dawn, who plays Vera Duckworth, Blair stopped outside the door of the house in Coronation Street where Vera and Jack live and pointed out that this was their house. With a little subterfuge, Blair was able to appear as though he was an avid fan.

There are plenty of politicians who have been caught out by not knowing the answers and seeming removed from everyday life. If you appear aloof, or from out of town, your opponents will use it against you, and may even invent stories to harm you like the famous one about Peter Mandelson in a northern fish 'n' chip shop pointing to mushy peas and asking for 'some of that guacamole' which can be traced back to the same story circulating about a US politician twenty years ago.

Background research

You need to know the facts and figures about the area you are contesting. If you are from outside the area, you should sit down with some local supporters and learn all the local knowledge you can: the main schools, hospitals, shopping centres, pubs and other amenities; the local campaigning groups and pressure groups, and the pronunciation of local place names.

From the library or your party headquarters you can get facts and figures about the local demographics – the age, occupation, ethnicity, type of home, car usage and so on – of your potential constituents.

You should also do some research on your opponents – finding out how they have voted on issues in the past, what business or commercial interests they have, what gaffes they have made in the past. You can research most people from the Internet, *Who's Who*, council minutes, local newspapers, and for MPs, *Hansard*. This 'Opposition Research' can prove very useful if they flip-flop on an issue or contradict themselves, or fail to fully declare all their interests such as company directorships. You should also investigate your opponent's Agent, and the ten people acting as their official nominators on their nomination form.

Polling and opinion research

Tony Blair once said that the most powerful person in the country is a member of a focus group, and he was only half joking. Focus groups have taken on mythological status in modern politics, but all they are really are groups of voters sitting around chatting while a facilitator asks them what they think about current events, political figures, policies or slogans. Their views are recorded, and usually video-taped, and analysed by experts. All political parties use them, and most politicians find their results useful.

Focus groups are just part of the picture. All politics should be based on an understanding of what people think and want they want. The politician who believes that they have their finger on the pulse of local opinion because they attend their local party meeting and hold regular surgeries is usually wide of the mark. The people who attend political meetings and go along to surgeries are not representative of local opinion. They may represent a strong current of opinion within an area, but they are unlikely to be in the majority.

The party meeting may be passionately concerned with Bosnia, or the Middle East. The surgery may be packed with people concerned about the Child Support Agency. The majority of voters may well be concerned with something else completely. The traditional methods for a politician to hear representations – party events, surgeries, public meetings – tend to be unrepresentative. Politicians like to think that they know what the people want, usually based on the flimsiest of evidence. The testimony of taxi-drivers, people on trains, barbers, and party activists is hardly a scientific basis for divining public opinion.

So modern campaigns are based on more sophisticated methods of researching public opinion. There are no perfect methods. Sometimes the politicians' instinct can be a truer guide than hard evidence. But modern research methods can play an important part for campaigners. These methods are the same that marketeers use to test research markets before product launches. They include quantitative research such as opinion polling, where large groups (more than 1000) are asked their views on certain issues, or tracking surveys, where the same groups are asked the questions over a period of time to track shifts in opinion, or qualitative research such as focus groups, where smaller groups of people are asked to explore issues at length, or share their views on political slogans, logos or figures.

Opinion polls showing the relative state of the parties' support and saliency are commissioned by newspapers and published monthly. During elections these become daily. The parties use their own private polling to guide their strategy. These might include tracking polls, 'bushfire polls' to test opinion on a new issue, or focus groups. In the USA, political campaigns often use 'push polls' which are designed to influence the electorate by asking biased and leading questions.

Polls are often wrong, which doesn't help their standing with politicians. In 1992, polls predicted a hung parliament. In 1997, the likely scale of Labour's landslide was not revealed by polling. 'Rogue' polls can show sudden changes in opinion which are an aberration. People lie to pollsters, and tell them what they think they should. People always say they want better public services, but vote for tax-cutting candidates. They even lie in 'Exit Polls', conducted after people have voted, and say they voted differently from the truth. The way to attempt to see an accurate picture is to cross-reference a variety of different polls over time.

Expenses and the deposit

Unlike in the USA, you are constrained by law in how much money you can spend on your campaign, and on what kind of activities. Only the candidate and their official agent can spend money on campaigning in a constituency, and the amount you can spend is determined by Parliament on the basis of a set amount plus an amount on top of that based on the number of electors. This works out at about £7-8,000. You cannot pay for someone to hand out leaflets or canvass voters or display posters for you. As the candidate you are not allowed to buy any drinks, meals or other gifts for other people during the campaign, as that might be construed as bribing or 'treating' the voters. The law ensures that local political campaigning is strictly amateur.

The great terror of candidates and their campaign teams is 'triggering their election expenses'. This means that the campaigning they are doing is deemed to have fired the starting pistol on the election. That is done by issuing material designed to attract votes for a particular candidate. Candidates must therefore avoid the word 'candidate' or even 'prospective' candidate until the election is called. To get round this, while still promoting the name of the candidate, parties invent job titles such as 'Labour's parliamentary spokesperson', 'Conservative campaign co-ordinator' or 'Liberal Democrat Focus Team'.

Each candidate must come up with a deposit – at the 2001 general election this was set at £700. If you are standing as a candidate for one of the main parties, the party will pay for your deposit. You 'save' your deposit if you win more than 5 per cent of the total number of votes cast (or 2.5 per cent in the European elections). You 'lose' your deposit if you fail to attract 5 per cent of the votes, as Tony Blair did at the Beaconsfield by-election in 1982. The money from lost deposits goes to the Treasury.

Nomination

There is one last task before you can launch your campaign – you must be nominated to stand as a candidate. This is not the same as being selected to stand under party colours. Getting nominated is the official process which means you are officially contesting the seat. The returning officer for each constituency issues nomination papers which must be returned by a certain date with the names and signatures of at least ten local people who are on the electoral register. This may rise to 50 in future elections. It is very important to get this right – to have the right number of people on the register and to get the papers in on time, otherwise you will not be able to stand in the election.

Before the campaign – a checklist
1 Make sure the candidate is clear what is expected – no cheering crowds and lots of hard work
2 Appoint an Agent
3 Find an HQ
4 Develop a plan – both strategy and tactics
5 Do your research and know your policies, and the price of milk
6 Motivate your volunteers and always say thank you
7 Pay attention to the impressions you create
8 Have enough money – at least for the deposit
9 Get the nomination in on time.

Part Two

THE SOUND OF GUNFIRE

'I intend to march my troops towards the sound of gunfire.'

Jo Grimond MP

Now you've done your preparation and research, you've drafted your Grid and your War Book. You are sure that your cause is just and your policies are right. Its time to reach the voters. It is time to march towards the sound of gunfire.

As we have seen, the result of the move in the UK to the Long Campaign and the Permanent Campaign is that many of the activities which were once confined to the month of an election campaign are now conducted all year round. Members of Parliament are seen as the catalyst for local campaigns, rather than as representatives in Westminster. During the 1997 Parliament, Labour MPs were given 'constituency weeks' when they would be sent back to their parliamentary constituencies to run local party campaigns. Because they have no chance of Ministerial office, Liberal Democrat MPs see their role as community activists and campaigners all year round. In marginal seats, the election campaign begins the day after Polling Day and lasts all Parliament.

Part of the modernisation of local councils has been to abolish the committee system and move the emphasis of local councillors' function away from the Town Hall and into the community. Some, such as Lewisham, have re-designated their back-bench councillors as 'front-line' councillors and encourage more campaigning work.

So campaigning activity is no longer confined to the four weeks of a campaign. It can be conducted using a variety of techniques all year round. Some of these campaign activities are as old as politics, some are brand new and will only be tested in future elections. They can be divided into 'direct' and 'indirect' or 'mediated' forms of campaigning.

'Direct' campaigning is where the candidate and party are in direct contact with voters, through:

personal meetings
street activity
canvassing
voter identification
blitzing
public meetings.

'Indirect' campaigning is where the voters are reached and the campaign is mediated via other channels of communication:

the media
advertising and posters
party election broadcasts
manifestos
leaflets and newsletters
direct mail
the Internet.

4   Direct Campaigning

Big smiles and firm handshakes

> 'The idea that you can merchandise candidates for high office like breakfast cereal ... is the ultimate indignity to the democratic process.'
>
> Adlai Stevenson

All campaigns will involve putting a candidate and a voter into direct contact. Here, the true mettle of the candidate is tested. The character of the candidate is put on show, without glossy leaflet or TV backdrop. The candidate is metaphorically naked. On a doorstep or in the high street, the candidate must be ready with a firm handshake, a big smile, and a friendly word or two. The encounter for the voter is a one-off; for the candidate, meeting each voter is one amongst thousands. The ability to stay alert, look interested, and keep on smiling through thousands of complaints and brickbats is an essential political skill. Few politicians succeed without being interested in what people have to say, and without being able to at least appear concerned about their troubles. Here the inner strength of the candidate is fully tested. Very few can fake sympathy and concern after weeks of constant campaigning, early starts leafleting railway stations and late nights in social clubs, and thousands of meetings with voters. When the tiredness sets in and the feet are aching, the true personality of the candidate comes through.

Great politicians have always got time for the voters. Harold Wilson could remember the names and concerns of nearly all the voters he met in his Huyton constituency over many years. Even when serving as Prime Minister, he would greet people in the streets of his constituency by name who he had met years before. The ability to store and recall peoples' names is as useful a political gift as any, and being remembered by your MP or councillor is flattering for voters.

Really famous politicians have to shake hands with thousands of people. Some learn the art of working crowds and shaking hundreds of hands per minute. Tony Blair uses a cross-over technique, whereby he can shake two people's hands at the same time as he moves down a crowd. In *Primary Colors*, Jack Stanton, the fictional candidate based on Bill Clinton, uses different handshakes with different people: a shake with the other hand on the elbow, or the biceps, or the shoulder, or the ultimate honour of a two-handed shake.

In 1991, Conservative Central Office advised its candidates to: 'shake hands with everybody, slap backs (where appropriate) take hold of arms (be gentle with the elderly, their joints hurt), pat shoulders, pat babies, pat dogs, stroke cats, make funny noises to budgerigars. Pressing the flesh is essential in any politician's armoury.'

It is hard to see how Conservatives could follow this advice without being arrested, but the point is well made. A big smile, a friendly quip, the use of the remembered first name, the slap on the back and the kiss for the baby can count for more in politics than your position on Europe or your grasp of tax policy.

Appearance

In 1955, the *Times* opined 'it will be an unfortunate day if it should come about that an election in this country is decided not by what either side says but by the way they looked while saying it.'

That unfortunate day has arrived. It is a sad fact that what candidates look like often matters more than what they stand for. Politicians have never been the most beautiful, sartorially-impressive social group – it has been said that 'politics is show-business for ugly people' – but in the age of 24-hour television and scrutiny, politicians' appearance has become increasingly salient. It is as if what clothes they wear and how they have their hair cut has become a metaphor for their strength of character and sense of their policies.

Michael Foot, leader of the Labour Party 1980–83, possesses one of the finest minds in politics. As a scholar, writer and journalist his contribution is impressive. In his day, he was one of the greatest orators. But all anyone can remember is *that* 'Donkey Jacket' worn to the Remembrance

Day service at the Cenotaph. Foot is adamant that it wasn't a Donkey Jacket, totem of CND marches and picket lines, but a perfectly sensible overcoat. The Queen Mother complimented him on his coat before the ceremony. But the media lambasted him for it, and few have forgotten the sartorial crime.

Part of Neil Kinnock's repositioning of the Labour Party after its defeats in the Eighties was to get the party to smarten up its act. Eighties Labour politicians, in their double-breasted suits, white shirts, regimental ties, and red rose button-holes bore little resemblance to their Seventies counterparts, in dungarees, sandals, *Atomkraft – Nein Danke* tee-shirts and beards. The Tories, with their City, business or Army backgrounds managed to scrub up reasonably well. Their grandees are known as 'the men in grey suits'. Labour's grandees of the past should have been the 'men in polyester suits'. Barbara Follett, now an MP, made her name by advising politicians on what colours and styles to go for to match their 'colouring'. Robin Cook was told to go for 'autumn colours' to complement his red hair. Most male politicians haven't a clue, their minds being on other more important matters, and rely on wives and secretaries to buy their *Liberty* ties and book their appointments at the barbers.

There has been speculation that baldness is a disadvantage in politics. In summer 2000, Neil Kinnock warned William Hague that bald men seldom become Prime Minister. Newspapers were filled with comment, and pictures of contemporary Prime Ministers from Lloyd George to Tony Blair, all with hair.

Even beards have come in for a hard time. Party strategists say beards are old-fashioned and make you look shifty. Some Labour politicians such as Alistair Darling have dispensed with their beards. It is said that Frank Dobson was advised by party strategists to get rid of his Father Christmas beard during the London Mayoral election, which he refused to do.

So what should a candidate look like? People expect their candidates to look smart. They expect a clean shirt or blouse, ladder-free tights and clean shoes. If out knocking on doors or appearing in public, the candidate should be wearing a suit, shirt and tie, or smart dress and jacket. The rule of thumb should be to wear what you would wear to a job interview, which is what an election campaign is – an extended job interview. But you should also be comfortable because electioneering is a tiring business. You should pay particular attention to your feet – and wear stout, comfortable shoes because during a campaign you will walk for many miles. There is a famous photograph of J. F. Kennedy during the 1960 election with the sole of his shoe worn right through with tramping the streets.

The old saying that you never get a second chance to make a first impression is truer of politics than anything else.

Canvassing and voter ID

Canvassing is perhaps the one activity which most people associate with local campaigning – candidates and their teams knocking on doors and talking to voters. That direct personal interaction is at the heart of a campaign. It connects politics with voters in the most naked of ways, and tears people away from the television or computer to confront the realities of elections – on their doorsteps and in their face. It provides no cover for spin or marketing – if your candidate has dandruff or a limp handshake, there is no hiding place. Canvassing is politics with the gloves off.

It should not be confused with the canvassing conducted by your council's electoral registration officers, who hire canvassers to get names onto the electoral register every year.

It can provide the canvasser with a disturbing insight into the psyche of the public, and the eccentricity, surprises and weirdness that is hidden behind the front doors of Britain. Any canvasser will know what I mean. As you tramp down unfamiliar streets and climb daunting staircases, you may daydream about meeting some gorgeous and available member of the public and being invited in to discuss the issues more fully, but in reality you are more likely to be confronted by a bewildered child, a hairy man in his vest, or some old Dot Cotton lookalike.

Canvassers, from all parties, have their own strange camaraderie, like birdwatchers or train-spotters, and will stop, even in the midst of a fierce by-election, to chat to one another. The bond between canvassers is an example of the adage that those involved in local politics have more in common with each other than with the voters.

Canvassing throws up funny anecdotes – tales of huge dogs, naked women and tattooed men. Steve Norris, the ex-MP and minister, tells the story of canvassing a house during the 1983 election. The door was

Please direct people to the Local Polling Station

(rg001) GOTV Pro-Labour Households

GOTV

	Constituency:	Anytown
	Ward:	CENTRAL
	Polling District:	AB
	Polling Station Address:	St Teresa's Primary School, High Street

Hopton Road

Poll #	Name	House	Phone	Voter id	Intended Voting Time
876	Bowen, Andrew S	18	02591 603467	Labour (firm)	
877	Bowen, Sheila A		02591 603467	Labour (firm)	
908	Simkin, Clare M	54	02591 603881	Target (Undecided - former Labour)	
909	Coates, Michael D		02591 603881	Target (Undecided - former Labour)	
930	Mirza, Hamair M	74	02591 751444	Labour (weak)	
931	Mirza, Nasreen		02591 751444	Labour (weak)	
939	Lee, Brenda	102	02591 751031	Labour (firm)	
967	Moore, Darren	158	02591 603031	Labour (firm)	
968	Coleman, Teresa		02591 603031	Labour (firm)	

GOTV – Getting Out The Vote is the most important part of polling day

answered by a scantily-clad woman, who invited him inside. The room was furnished from ceiling to floor in black leather, and inside was another negligée-wearing woman and a huge bloke with gold teeth. 'What do you want?' asked the man. 'I'm canvassing for the Conservative candidate and I was wondering whether we can count on your support', said Norris. 'Conservative, are you?' said the man 'That's all right, we're all in favour of small businesses round here, aren't we girls?'

Many voters make the mistake of assuming that political canvassers are knocking on their doors, like Jehovah's Witnesses, to try to convert them. The purpose of canvassing is not to try to convert voters, or argue with them about politics, but to identify how they intend to vote. Sometimes voters are disappointed when canvassers walk away from an argument. Knowing how

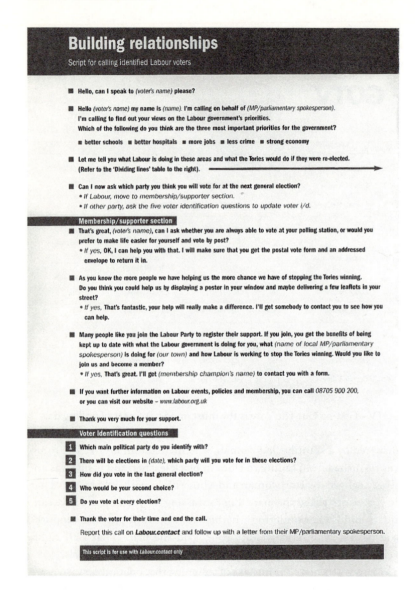

Building relationships

Script for calling identified Labour voters

- **Hello, can I speak to** *(voter's name)* **please?**

- **Hello** *(voter's name)* **my name is** *(name)*. **I'm calling on behalf of** *(MP/parliamentary spokesperson)*. **I'm calling to find out your views on the Labour government's priorities. Which of the following do you think are the three most important priorities for the government?**

    ■ **better schools** ■ **better hospitals** ■ **more jobs** ■ **less crime** ■ **strong economy**

- **Let me tell you what Labour is doing in these areas and what the Tories would do if they were re-elected. (Refer to the 'Dividing lines' table to the right).** ➡

- **Can I now ask which party you think you will vote for at the next general election?**
    • *If Labour, move to membership/supporter section.*
    • *If other party, ask the five voter identification questions to update voter i/d.*

Membership/supporter section

- **That's great,** *(voter's name)*, **can I ask whether you are always able to vote at your polling station, or would you prefer to make life easier for yourself and vote by post?**
    • *If yes*, OK, I can help you with that. I will make sure that you get the postal vote form and an addressed envelope to return it in.

- **As you know the more people we have helping us the more chance we have of stopping the Tories winning. Do you think you could help us by displaying a poster in your window and maybe delivering a few leaflets in your street?**
    • *If yes*, That's fantastic, your help will really make a difference. I'll get somebody to contact you to see how you can help.

- **Many people like you join the Labour Party to register their support. If you join, you get the benefits of being kept up to date with what the Labour government is doing for you, what** *(name of local MP/parliamentary spokesperson)* **is doing for** *(our town)* **and how Labour is working to stop the Tories winning. Would you like to join us and become a member?**
    • *If yes*, That's great. I'll get *(membership champion's name)* to contact you with a form.

- **If you want further information on Labour events, policies and membership, you can call** 08705 900 200, **or you can visit our website –** www.labour.org.uk

- **Thank you very much for your support.**

Voter identification questions

1 **Which main political party do you identify with?**

2 **There will be elections in** *(date)*, **which party will you vote for in these elections?**

3 **How did you vote in the last general election?**

4 **Who would be your second choice?**

5 **Do you vote at every election?**

- **Thank the voter for their time and end the call.**

    Report this call on ***Labour.contact*** and follow up with a letter from their MP/parliamentary spokesperson.

    This script is for use with *Labour.contact* only

Telephone canvassing scripts

Dividing lines

operation*turnout*

new **Labour**
new **Britain**

Labour
is investing in:

Schools
- cutting class sizes for five, six and seven-year-olds
- giving thousands of pounds to every school for books and equipment
- improving standards of literacy and numeracy.

Hospitals
- delivering 20,000 extra nurses and 200 more GPs
- providing 7,000 extra beds
- building 100 new hospital developments
- cutting waiting lists.

Employment
- putting one million more people back to work, with the help of the New Deal
- given 1.7 million people a pay rise with the minimum wage
- given holiday rights and better conditions to all workers.

Crime
- cutting the arrest-to-sentence time for young offenders
- reducing the number of burglaries and car crimes
- giving extra money to recruit more police officers and tackle crime.

The economy
- created the conditions for strong, sustained economic growth
- cutting taxes for hard-working families
- delivering lower interest rates and lower mortgages.

The Tories
are committed to policies which would cut spending by £24 million in our area which would:

Schools
- increase class sizes for your children
- cut Labour's extra money for schools
- axe teachers and lower standards.

Hospitals
- cut the number of doctors and nurses
- make people go private for operations like cataract removals and hip replacements
- cancel Labour's new hospital developments
- make people wait longer for operations.

Employment
- cancel the New Deal and put more people back on the dole
- undermine the minimum wage, giving millions of people a pay cut
- cancel the better conditions that Labour has delivered for workers.

Crime
- catch fewer criminals
- make your community less safe by allowing crime to rise
- axe the extra money that Labour is spending to cut crime.

The economy
- go back to boom and bust, and economic failure
- increase taxes for the many and cut taxes for the privileged few
- increase interest rates making mortgages more expensive.

Specific information about your constituency can be found at

www.labour.org.uk

105/2K Published by the Labour Party, Millbank Tower, Millbank, London SW1P 4GT
Printed by HN Associates, City House, Sutton Park Road, Sutton, Surrey SM1 2AE

Labour
www.labour.org.uk

voters intend to vote is essential information for local campaigns. Voters' names and addresses are gathered from the Electoral Register, published each year constituency-by-constituency.

Canvassing also identifies those of your supporters who need an Absentee Vote – either a postal vote or a proxy vote – because they will be unable to vote on polling day in person because of illness, work, or because they are away from home. Postal votes are an important part of your pre-election work, because they represent votes already cast for you. In 1992 in Cambridge, the 5000 postal votes, mostly students, were enough to win Labour the seat from the Tories.

Parties can cross-reference the new register with their existing records from previous elections and see who has moved, and how many of their supporters are still at the same address and registered to vote. The 'marked register' is available from the Town Hall which shows, by the names crossed out, who voted at the last national or local election, and forms the basis of canvassing in the next election.

The information gathered – the 'canvass returns' – is centralised for each ward and each constituency and analysed. Canvass returns allow local campaign HQs, or committee rooms, usually in someone's front room or kitchen, to mark up an electoral register with the voting intentions of all the voters in a particular area. Those who have promised to vote for you (the 'promise') are those who you try to get out to vote on polling day.

The traditional system of canvassing is the Reading system, developed by the Reading constituency Labour Party and its MP, Ian Mikardo, in the 1945 election. This involved the centralisation of accurate information about voters' intentions in central Committee Rooms, with the Labour voters identified on 'Reading pads' pasted onto a long table or plank of wood. These were address-by-address lists of Labour voters with identical copies underneath. On polling day, the sheets were torn off the pads and given to activists to knock up the voters. At each polling station, the individual number of each voter, stated on the Polling Card, is given to the number takers from the parties.

Here, number takers from different parties will sit together, sometimes for hours, and chat, while sharing the numbers as the voters come through the system. Every hour, the numbers are collected from the 'teller pads' and fed back to the Committee Rooms, and those who have voted are crossed off the lists of the 'promised vote'. That means that as each sheet is torn off the Reading pads, it should contain only the names of voters who have not yet voted. Computer databases have helped the process. The Tories use a near-identical system where voters are identified as C for conservative, D for doubtful, S for Socialist (Labour), L for Liberal Democrat and A for against, but would not say more.

Labour pioneered Elpack, which allowed canvass returns to be databased, but has recently moved to a remarkable system called **Labour.contact**, which is a windows-based software package which allows long-term relationships to be maintained from election to election by storing a range of information on individuals.

Telephone canvassing is the logical development of door-to-door canvassing. Voters are contacted by phone, using the telephone directory to collate the numbers of voters on the electoral register. There is resistance to the idea of telephone canvassing in some more traditionalist quarters because of its connotations of double-glazing or fitted-kitchen sales techniques.

It was the Tories who pioneered telephone canvassing in the eighties as an effective communications device. Their latest development is GENEVA, a new telephone canvassing system based at Conservative Central Office, which allocates volunteers on the phone bank names and numbers of key swing voters anywhere in the country, and a script to follow on a computer screen. The Tories' opponents in elections would say 'haven't seen much of the Tories on the streets' and then go on to lose. The Tory activists would have spent their time in central phone 'banks', with a carefully crafted telephone script, contacting many thousands more voters than the traditional door-to-door approach.

The logical development is 'cyber-canvassing' – canvassing online, via chatrooms, emails and the Internet.

Voter Identification
The Labour Party has developed its system of canvassing into a sophisticated series of categories, each identified by a code letter against the name on the register – called 'voter i/d'.

Voter i/d allows voters in target areas to be communicated with according to their voting intention, but with more information than simple 'for or against'. Labour can target 'weak Labour' voters with one message via direct mail or leaflets, and 'weak Tory' voters with another. Messages can be honed for those who voted Labour last time, but are unsure whether to vote Labour next time, or those who voted Tory last time, but have told canvassers that they might vote Labour next time. Some people are voting for the first time, especially those who have attained their majority (ie turned 18) since the last election, and they will have appropriate communication from the parties.

Labour began its programme of voter i/d three years before the 1997 general election, unlike traditional canvassing which takes place close to an election. The contact with voters is closely scripted, so that voters all over the country are being asked the same set of questions. In the period leading up to the 1997 election the Labour script ran as follows:

- Which party do you most closely identify with?
- Who are you going to vote for in the forthcoming election?
- Who did you vote for at the last election?
- Who would be your second choice?
- Do you always vote, or sometimes vote?

Labour then segmented the voters into the following categories:

- strong Labour voters – who vote Labour and vote at all elections
- weak Labour voters – who always vote Labour but do not always vote at every election
- Tory switchers – people who intended to vote Labour but voted Tory last time
- Liberal/Nationalist 'squeeze' voters – voters who would vote Labour as their second choice
- Those who were undecided, wouldn't say, or voted Tory.

This allows accurate tailoring of messages to each group. For example, Dennis Skinner MP, the favourite of traditional Labour voters, would be used to contact strong Labour voters in certain seats, but in others, the Tory switchers would be contacted by a prominent Tory defector such as Alan Howarth or Shaun Woodward.

This form of personal contact with voters only works if enough voters can be contacted. Labour's campaign in 1997 involved an 80 per cent 'contact rate' with voters in the key 91 battle-ground seats, meaning that 80 per cent of voters in those seats had a personal contact from a Labour volunteer.

Modern technology means that parties can develop detailed databases of information on the voters and seek to forge a more personal relationship with them than the traditional mass communications of posters, broadcasts and uniform canvassing.

Blitzing

Blitzing is a technique developed by Labour during the string of by-elections in the mid and late 1990s. It is designed to maximise the exposure of the party candidate and leading party figures to local voters in as short a time as possible, so that more ground can be covered than traditional canvassing. It does not allow for fireside chats and discussion of the issues – it requires speed and energy.

Blitzing is focused on areas with historically low turnout, and is designed to inject some excitement and energy into an area. Teams of volunteers knock on doors down each side of the street, and find voters who would like to meet the candidate. The volunteer then stands with an arm in the air so that the team around the candidate knows which house to visit. The candidate is rushed down the street meeting those voters who are in, and want to meet them, thus reaching people in a far more efficient way than traditional canvassing.

Blitzing, especially during a by-election, can work well with a well-known political figure. I took part in some blitzing in the South East Staffordshire by-election in 1996 with John Prescott. My job was to use the megaphone attached to the top of a car to invite voters to 'come and meet John Prescott, Labour's deputy leader' and they did.

Street activity

Your campaign should include high visibility work in centres of population: high streets, shopping centres, railway stations, bus stations and so on. Street campaigning can reach a lot of people in a short space of time.

Collecting signatures for a petition

It is used for reinforcing messages and being seen, rather than collecting information that is directly relevant to voter identification. You can set up a street stall using a portable decorators' table and a covering.

Your stall can include leaflets and brochures, membership forms, and information about the candidate. You might use a petition as a way of engaging the voters and collecting names and addresses of potential supporters. You can even campaign with some kind of stunt. In 1997, Labour candidates bought a basket of shopping with the equivalent amount of money that they claimed the government were taking per week from the average family. The shopping was displayed with the slogan – 'this is what you could have had every week without the Tory tax rises.' It drew people in – probably because they thought it was the prize in a raffle.

In some parts of your constituency, such as shopping centres, you may need permission to distribute leaflets. You must always ensure that you do not block the thoroughfare or cause any nuisance, especially to local traders. You need to be seen, but not in the way.

As well as street activity like leafleting, petitioning, stunts and so on, you should try to have a presence at other community events like fetes, summer fairs, and jumble sales.

Getting out the vote

In an age of apathy, election campaigns are as much geared to persuading people to get out to vote as they are to persuading people *how* to vote. Get Out the Vote (or GOTV) activity used to involve a van and a megaphone driving around the areas where you knew your supporters lived, and making enough racket to get them out of the house. It was not much more sophisticated than the 'knockers up' who went down the street tapping on the bedroom windows of factory workers with a long pole at the crack of dawn to wake them for their day's work. (For US readers, I know that 'knocking up' means something quite different in the American context!)

The van and megaphone is still employed in modern campaigns, especially in areas of concentrated support. Campaigns are issued with tapes with music and politicians' voice-overs to save the lungs of local campaigners, and which give the impression that William Hague or John Prescott is in a car outside your house asking you to vote. The tapes are on a loop, so that whoever is in the car driving around must suffer hours of the same two-minute burst of speech and music over and over again. In 1997, most Labour campaigners never wanted to hear 'Things can only get better' ever again.

On polling day, the job is to get your supporters out to vote.

Campaigners are sent out from the time the polls open until the last minute, knocking on doors. Lists of voters who have told canvassers they will vote for your party are issued, and the competition becomes one to see which side can be more efficient at getting their supporters to the polling stations. Lists include names, addresses, phone numbers, and voter i/d information such as whether they are strong or weak supporters. Your information may also include information about what time they intend to vote, such as before or after work, and whether they need a lift in a car to the polling station.

Each party appoints 'polling agents' who attend polling stations on election day and try to ensure that the election is being conducted within the rules. The polling agents look out for electoral malpractice

Election day literature

such as *personation*, where one person tries to vote using the name of another, or obstruction of the ballot.

Elections are won on turnout, and in close elections they are won in the last hour of polling day. That is why a high contact rate is essential, so that you know where your supporters are, and can carry on squeezing them out of their homes until the polls close, whilst your opponents are twiddling their thumbs. For example, Luke Akehurst, former Labour organiser in London and now a parliamentary candidate, says 'for a local election you should aim for a 70 per cent contact rate, and aim to get double the number of promised votes than you actually need to win the ward, because not everyone will vote. You can keep getting votes all day – and if your organisation is better than the enemy's, you will win the seat.'

Top tips for contact with the voters

1 Accurate canvassing and effective GOTV can win elections
2 Make your efforts count – target the areas where the election will be decided
3 Blitz areas with low turnout
4 Get the postal votes in the bag
5 Don't waste time chatting on the doorsteps
6 Don't send canvassers out on their own after dark
7 Don't let the candidate get into arguments and debates

8 Let people see you – get out into the high streets and shopping centres with street stalls, petitions, balloons and leaflets
9 Keep going until the polls close, never give up
10 Have a party afterwards to unwind and say thank you.

Hustings and meetings

Public political meetings are becoming a rare event. Some public meetings, if they concern a matter of urgent local concern such as a new incinerator or supermarket, can attract hundreds of citizens. Question and Answer sessions conducted by Ministers or Prime Ministers can attract healthy-sized audiences, usually by invitation only. But the public meeting to let the local voters hear the competing claims of local politicians belongs to the days of the wireless and *Picture Post*.

There are exceptions. Jack Straw MP organised 'Shout-about' sessions in the town square in his Blackburn constituency, where he would stand on a soap box and take on all comers. Other local campaigners, usually on the left of the spectrum, use street corner soapbox and megaphone campaign methods.

During an election, there will be some local meetings, and perhaps hustings between candidates, often organised by the local churches or community groups, so the candidate needs to know what to expect and how to handle a public meeting.

Making a speech

'A democracy is no more than an aristocracy of orators.'

Thomas Hobbes

Candidates have to make speeches. From the moment you stand for selection as a candidate, to your speech on the night of the election count, you will be expected to be able to make speeches on a variety of occasions. Some will be set-piece debates with your opponents, some speeches to the party faithful, others off-the-cuff remarks while drawing the winners at the fundraising raffle or after dinner. Speech-making is a dying art in politics. The quality of content and delivery has declined as other forms of communication, especially television, have taken over election campaigning. But we still live in a political culture where a good speech matters.

Peggy Noonan, speech-writer to Ronald Reagan, says: 'A speech is part theatre and part political declaration; it is personal communication between a leader and his people; it is art, and all art is a paradox, being at once a thing of great power and great delicacy. A speech is poetry: cadence, rhythm, imagery, sweep. A speech reminds us that words, like children, have the power to make dance the dullest beanbag of a heart ... they count. They more than count, they shape what happens.'

Many phrases which sum up historical themes are made in the course of a speech and strike a chord in the popular consciousness: Churchill's description of an 'iron curtain' descending across Europe in the depths of the Cold War, Kennedy's 'new frontier' during the space race in the 1960s, Harold Macmillan's 'winds of change' sweeping through post-colonial Africa. Even at the local level, a particular campaign theme or message can be reiterated through speech-making during a campaign.

The power of rhetoric can be used to provoke base instincts and hatreds: Adolf Hitler's speeches at Nuremberg, or Enoch Powell's 'Rivers of Blood' speech in 1968. It can be used to make the spirit soar, make us laugh or cry, inspire us to action and persuade us of a case. It is a powerful gift for a politician to possess. Some politicians are famous for it. Michael Foot said of Aneurin Bevan: 'Bevan wrought an alchemy before our eyes. He could mix fire with ice. He could evoke dreams and the boldest aspirations, yet the purpose always was to use the motive force thus generated to help forward the business in hand.' Disraeli said of Gladstone: 'A sophisticated rhetorician, inebriated with the exuberance of his own verbosity.'

The leader of the 1889 Great Dock Strike in London, Ben Tillett, was a small man who suffered from a stammer. Yet he overcame his stammer and nerves to become an inspiring orator who could motivate great crowds to action. One contemporary said of Tillett: 'He was small in size and he seemed insignificant until he got up to speak. Then he seemed to grow in stature and he had a voice of silver. He could stir the emotions of a crowd with almost incomparable virtuosity. He could make it laugh with him and weep with him. He could set it on fire with passionate indignation.'

Even in the age of webcasts and television, today's political leaders are expected to possess the same gifts for oratory as the leaders of the Roman senate or Victorian Westminster. William Hague and Tony Blair spend weeks preparing for their speeches at their annual party conferences. They are practised and tested and re-drafted. Every word is designed for an effect. There are no wandering passages or extraneous verbiage. A Leader's character and proficiency is tested against their ability to please their audience. When it goes wrong, as happened to Tony Blair during his ill-advised address to the Women's Institute in summer 2000, it reflects badly on the speaker.

So it is worth putting in the work to get it right.

Preparing your speech

Very, very few speakers speak genuinely 'off-the-cuff'. To give the appearance of a few well-chosen words, effortlessly delivered, requires real skill and training. The shorter the time you have, the harder it is to construct your speech. Churchill used to say that if he had to speak for an hour, he would spend five minutes preparing himself, but if he had to speak for five minutes, he would spend many hours. American President Woodrow Wilson said: 'If I am to speak for ten minutes I need a week for preparation. If fifteen minutes, three days. If half an hour, two days. If an hour, I am ready now.'

When big-hitting politicians have to make a speech, the process can take months and involve a cast of thousands. So you should always prepare your speech, no matter how confident you may be.

Using notes

Different speakers prefer different ways of keeping their notes. Some prefer bullet points on a series of index cards, others prefer the speech to be written out in full on A4 paper.

There is a story that Denis Healey (or possibly Edward Heath, depending on which version you hear) had been behaving insufferably to his civil service team in the lead-up to a major speech, and they decide to have their revenge. After the speech is thrust into the hands of the Minister, he stands up at the major conference to deliver the unseen text.

All is going well. The Minister is regaling his audience with facts and statistics, when suddenly, as he turns to page 14, the speech comes to an abrupt halt. The Minister stares at a blank page. All the rest of the pages are blank. At the top is a hand-written note: 'From now on Minister, you're on your own.'

Reconnaissance

If at all possible you should try to see the room or hall you will be speaking in beforehand. You should stand at the lectern, look into the space where your audience will be, make the walk from the chair to the place you will deliver the speech from, checking for steps or electrical cables which might impede your journey, and feel as comfortable as possible about the environment. You should check the background for any hostages to fortune (for example, signs saying 'Way Out'). Make sure the lectern and microphone is the right height for you. Try turning the microphone on and off, so that you do not fiddle around on the night.

Before the meeting, meet the chair, and check that he has your name and title correct. He or she will be introducing you to the meeting, and so you want to make sure they get your name right. When the veteran Welsh politician Leo Abse (pronounced Ab-see) was a young candidate, the chairman of a meeting in the valleys was giving him a fulsome introduction as the young man with a great future, but kept pronouncing his name incorrectly, with only one syllable. Eventually the embarrassed young hopeful whispered to the chairman 'Call me Abse'. The chairman announced: 'you see ladies and gentlemen – our new candidate has just told me we should call him Ab-see. What a friendly chap – from now on, you can call me Jones-y.'

The chair may also want a few biographical details about you, and what you intend to talk about. Make sure that you both agree on how long you have to speak and how long for questions afterwards, and if there is more than one speaker, agree which order you will speak in.

Style and delivery

The style and delivery of your speech must match the type of meeting, the size of audience, who the audience is, and the subject you are discussing. There is nothing worse than a politician addressing a meeting of six people as though it was a rally of ten thousand, or vice versa.

There are various tried and tested tools in the speech-makers toolkit which can be used. The truly great speeches from history, many of which are available on CD, teach us about some of the ways to make a speech work, and there are techniques and rhetorical devices which you can use:

Groups of Three

Try using 'groups of three'. Many of the most famous phrases throughout history are groups of three. Groups of three satisfy most peoples' need for unity and closure; they work at a subconscious level. Just think of these famous examples:

- Father, Son and Holy Ghost (The Bible)
- Bread, Peace, and Land (Lenin)
- Ein Volk, Ein Reich, Ein Führer (Hitler)
- Of the people, by the people, for the people (Abraham Lincoln)
- A Mars a day helps you work, rest and play (The Mars Company)
- Education, Education, Education (Tony Blair).

You can use groups of three to set out your demands or campaign issues during speeches.

Repetition

Repetition can be used to give a speech a lyrical, poetic quality. By repeating the same phrase within the passage of a speech, the point is made stronger and will live in the audiences' memory.

On 4 June 1940, Winston Churchill made this famous address, repeating 'we shall fight' over and over again:

'We shall fight in France/we shall fight on the seas and oceans/we shall fight with growing confidence and growing strength in the air/ we shall defend our island/ whatever the cost shall be/we shall fight on the beaches/ we shall fight on the landing grounds/we shall fight in the fields and in the streets/we shall fight in the hills/we shall never surrender.'

And no-one could have doubted what the message was.

On 28 August 1963 in Washington DC, 250,000 people heard Martin Luther King make his 'I have a dream' speech. He repeated the phrase 'I have a dream' five times, and the phrase 'Let freedom ring' nine times in the space of ten minutes.

In Neil Kinnock's speech delivered on the eve of Mrs Thatcher's second general election victory in 1983, he repeated the refrain 'I warn you' fourteen times in the space of a few minutes, culminating in: 'If Mrs Thatcher wins – I warn you not to be ordinary/I warn you not to be young/I warn you not to fall ill/I warn you not to get old.'

In his 1999 and 2000 Labour Party conference speeches, Gordon Brown used repetition for comic effect, repeating certain phrases and getting the audience to join in.

Imagery

You can use imagery to liven up your speech and engage the audience. For example, Churchill's 'Give us the tools and we will finish the job' or Aneurin Bevan's 'If you carry this resolution you will send Britain's Foreign Secretary naked into the conference chamber' or 'Why read the crystal when he can read the book?', or Norman Tebbit's 'He did not riot – he got on his bike and looked for work.'

Self-effacement

Audiences quite like speakers to show a little humility and self-effacement, no matter how egotistical they may be under the surface. The old cliché of the speaker starting with the caveat 'Unaccustomed as I am to public speaking ... ' is an example of the device. Or how about this, from Shakespeare: 'I am no orator as Brutus is. But, as you know me all, a plain, blunt man, that love'd my friend.'

Quotations

A quote from a political hero can imply that you agree with them, or even that you want your audience to identify you with them. Labour politicians will quote heroes like Aneurin Bevan or Keir Hardie, Liberals will use Lloyd George, no Tory is without a stock of quotes from Churchill or Thatcher. Within political parties, a quote can imply on which side of the fence you stand on an issue. No Blairite will use Karl Marx to help their arguments; few Tory Euro-sceptics will quote Edward Heath. Some of the great orators have used quotes in their rhetoric, for example Leo Amery quoting the words of Cromwell in the emergency debate in 1940

'In the name of God, go!' or Enoch Powell quoting 'The Roman' in his Rivers of Blood speech in 1968.

Jokes

Humour is a tricky one to pull off in a speech. A few self-depreciating works or a jibe at your opponent's expense can work well enough, but full-scale joke-telling requires real skill. Anyone who has acted as a Best Man has probably managed to get a laugh from their audience, but at a wedding everyone is on your side. A political audience is highly discerning, and less likely to laugh out of loyalty or a desire to see you succeed. There are some good political jokes which can be used as stand-bys for after-dinner speeches, or ones which can be used to illustrate a political point.

Here's one that the IPPR's Matthew Taylor told at a recent conference to illustrate the point that the voters, no matter what governments do for them, are an ungrateful bunch:

A woman is sitting with her baby son on the beach, when from nowhere there's a clap of thunder and a huge tidal wave crashes onto the beach and sweeps her son out to sea.

Fearing that he is lost forever, the woman goes down on her knees and starts praying to God 'Oh Lord, please return my son, and I will never doubt you again, and I will serve you for the rest of my days.'

There's another clap of thunder, and another huge tidal wave deposits her son back on the beach, safe and sound.

'Oh Lord, thank you,' says the woman. 'But there's just one more thing – he was wearing a hat!'

This one is about the legendary drunkard politician George Brown:

George Brown, 'tired and emotional' as usual, is at some splendid diplomatic function at Carlton House Gardens, when through the crowd he spots a resplendent figure in crimson. He sidles up and says 'My dear, the band are playing a waltz, would you care to join me on the dance floor?'

Comes the answer: 'Mr Brown I will not dance with you for three reasons:

Firstly, you are drunk;

Secondly, this is not a waltz it is the national anthem of my country;
And thirdly, I am the Cardinal Archbishop of Lima!'

Here's another:

The New Labour candidate meets Peter Mandelson and then spends the rest of the day being the perfect candidate whilst all the time wearing a Sony Walkman. Later in the day he goes for a new Labour haircut, but because of the long day he falls asleep in the chair.

The barber removes the headphones to cut the hair and several minutes later the candidate dies in the chair. The understandably concerned barber picks up the headphones and hears Peter Mandelson's voice saying 'breathe in ... breathe out ... breathe in'.

Or this one:

The Party Leader and the Deputy Party Leader are on an election walkabout in a fairly rural town. They and their entourage, including supporters and journalists, come upon a so-called wishing well. The Party Leader, conscious of the photo opportunity at election time, leans over the well, makes a wish, and, beaming at the cameras, throws in a coin.

The Deputy Leader, not to be outdone, decides to make a wish as well. Unfortunately, leaning over too far, the Deputy Leader falls down into the well screaming. The well turns out to be hundreds of feet deep and it is clear to all those present that the unfortunate deputy has been killed instantly.

The Party Leader stands there shaken for a moment, but is aware that, in an election, a dramatic situation like this calls for an appropriate political response, and thinking on his feet, quickly exclaims to the assembled aides and reporters, 'My God! It works!'

Jokes can be caustic and make a point:

Question: If Michael Ashcroft, Jeffrey Archer and Archie Norman jump from a plane at 20,000 feet without a parachute – who survives?
Answer: The Conservative Party.

It is worth making a note of jokes as you hear them, and having a stock ready for any occasion. You should also try to remember which joke you've told to which audience, so that you avoid the humiliation of starting to tell a joke, as Michael Portillo did once, everyone has heard you tell them before.

Anecdotes

Anecdotes are another useful part of the armoury. These need not be chat-show style funny stories; they can be serious. An anecdote about a real person or family, perhaps one you've met during the campaign, can be used to illustrate a serious political point and make some policy or statistic come alive. Audiences can relate to real people, and understand complex political issues through their effect on peoples' lives. In Joe Klein's *Primary Colors,* the fictional US Presidential Candidate, Jack Stanton, has an anecdote for every occasion. When visiting an adult literacy class, he tells the story of his Uncle Charlie who had won the congressional medal of honour in the Second World War, but lacked the courage to admit he couldn't read or write. It turns out the story is made up, but long after the Governor's audience has applauded him to the rafters.

Rhetorical questions

A rhetorical question is a device to make the audience think and to follow a line of argument. It works because questions demand answers, and so an audience is engaged for as long as the circle remains unclosed. It establishes a riddle, and allows the speaker to resolve it. Neil Kinnock's speech in Llandudno on 15 May 1987 during the election campaign, repeated later in the famous 'Kinnock, the Movie' party election broadcast, was structured almost entirely around rhetorical questions, starting with the famous, and copied, demand: 'Why am I the first Kinnock in a thousand generations to be able to get to university? Why is Glenys the first woman in her family to get to university? Was it because all our predecessors were "thick"?

Were those people not university material? Couldn't they have knocked off all their A levels in an afternoon?

Was it because they were weak? – those people who could work eight hours underground and then come up and play football? Weak? Those women who could survive eleven child bearings, were they weak?'

This passage of the speech leads the listener to ask why, to become outraged that they were denied the opportunities. Finally Kinnock answers the questions he has been firing at his audience: 'It was because there was no platform on which they could stand.'

The American politician Joe Biden later stole the device in a speech, and asked 'Why am I the fourteenth Joe Biden ...?' but was exposed as a copy-cat.

Your hands and body language

The way you use your hands and your body language can have a huge impact on the way your audience receives your speech. You need to be aware of what your limbs are up to during your speech, and control their activity. You should always stand up to make a speech, stand straight, and hold your head up. You have far more freedom of expression than appearing on television or radio, but you must still try to keep things in proportion.

You should not lose your eye-contact with your audience by looking down at your notes, or worse, holding your speech in front of your face. You can fix an imaginary point on the wall at the back of the hall, and keep looking up at that. Skilled speakers will allow their gaze to rove across all parts of the audience, making eye-contact with different people in the audience, so that for a few seconds, each person in the audience thinks they are being addressed in person.

You can use your hands to add rhetorical effect, but be careful not to allow wild flourishes or extravagant gestures to detract from your arguments. Hand movements must be controlled and rationed. You can grasp the lectern if there is one, or place them on the table in front of you. You can grasp your lapels for a 'Victorian statesman' effect. One hand can be held up, palm open, and used to measure out a particular point. An appeal can be made by both hands, palm open, towards the audience. You can beat out a point by punching the flat of your left hand with the clenched right. Tony Blair uses this technique. You can use a pointed index figure, but never aim at anyone in particular – that is threatening and rude. You can even bang the top of the table to introduce some passion and excitement to a speech.

Props

Speakers often like to use props to illustrate their point or to help give them confidence and add to their speech. The term 'prop' is borrowed from the world of the theatre, and means a physical object which is deployed to aid your performance.

The most common prop is a lectern, behind which the speaker can feel protected and secure. The lectern can be used as a rest for your speech notes, and a place to put your hands in between rhetorical gestures. Lecterns can be adorned with the logo and name of the organisation which is hosting the event, or the venue where the event is taking place.

A glass of water is a useful prop. It has the duel purpose of being useful to keep the mouth lubricated during a speech, and also as a way of buying time during questions. A sip from the glass of water can buy valuable seconds when formulating the answer to a tricky or unwelcome question.

Some speakers use their spectacles as a prop. They can be taken off, which implies a breaking down of barriers and honesty. They can be folded, and used as a pointer to emphasis a particular point of your argument. During the 2000 US Presidential election debates, George W. Bush offered to lend his glasses to a member of the audience who couldn't find hers to read out her question.

The older generation of politicians, before smoking in public was deemed unacceptable, would use their pipes as a prop. Harold Wilson and Tony Benn are two examples. Baroness Falkender, Harold Wilson's long-time assistant has observed that 'pipes, in politics, are extremely useful: they can be filled, lit, tamped down or sucked while the owner is thinking out a reply to a tricky question; they can be waved about for emphasis, or they can be sucked slowly to give a reassuring, thoughtful and trustworthy effect.'

Props might be designed to shock your audience. A speech on human rights abuses might involve a prop like a real plastic bullet. Speeches against animal cruelty might use the metal teeth of an animal trap. The Welsh MP Ann Clwyd brought the casing from a shell into the Chamber of the House of Commons to make a point about Iraq's suppression of the Kurds, despite props being strictly forbidden from parliamentary debates. A speech on world hunger can use a handful of rice which millions of people have to survive on every day.

You can use props for humorous effect – a blank sheet of paper can be shown to illustrate your opponent's new ideas for the constituency or what they have done for local people. In 1995, John Prescott used a pork pie on a silver platter at Labour Party conference to show the 'pork pies' he claimed the Tories had been telling ('Pork pies' = 'lies' in cockney rhyming slang).

Technical equipment

The eighties saw the arrival of 'sincerity machines' – one-way glass panels in which the speaker can see the text of his speech, but which the audience can see straight through. An assistant in a remote location scrolls through the speech electronically, in the same way a television presenter reads from an autocue.

This allows politicians to give the appearance of maintaining eye contact with his or her audience by keeping their head up and panning the audience, but actually they are reading off a script. The panels are unobtrusive and cannot be easily detected by a television audience. Margaret Thatcher pioneered their use in Britain, and now politicians regularly use them for big speeches.

Sincerity machines confer enormous power to the person scrolling through the speech. The opportunity for a disgruntled apparatchik to cause a major politician to appear to slow down, speed up, or stop altogether has not yet to my knowledge been exercised, but the opportunity remains. It is a very foolhardy politician who relies completely on the machine and appears on a platform without a back-up copy of his or her speech in a pocket. It was rumoured that Gordon Brown's barnstorming speech to the 1999 Labour conference was helped by a technical failure of the sincerity machine, which meant the politician had to rely on old-fashioned tub-thumping oratory, and the conference loved it.

Dealing with hecklers

Like a good stand-up comedian, a politician can turn a heckler into an ally. A speech can be given new impetus and excitement by the timely intervention of a heckler, and the skill with which the heckler is dispatched can prove what a quick-witted and skilled player the politician is. Some politicians thrive on hecklers, and some even 'plant' hecklers to give their speeches an edge.

But not all heckling is welcome. There might be attempts from members of the audience to disrupt the meeting or destabilise the speakers. This might be from individuals, or part of a co-ordinated group. Political speakers are seen as fair game for dirty tricks.

Experienced speakers are used to dealing with hecklers – they ignore them, or have an armoury of put-downs to shut them up and win over the audience. ('I see we have the Young Conservatives/Socialists in tonight', 'Are you from the Womens' Institute?' etc.)

If the speaker is interrupted or loses their flow, the chairman might have to step in and ask for order and request that the heckler be quiet. The audience usually sides with a strong chairman in these situations. If the heckler continues, the stewards should step in, if there are any, and request that the heckler be quiet and sit down. As a last resort, the person can be asked to leave the hall.

If a group of opponents really want to disrupt your meeting and co-ordinate their tactics, they will usually succeed. Some political groups on the extreme right or left want to disrupt public meetings. All that can be done is for the chair to make it clear to the audience who is to blame for the disruption, and close the meeting.

Taking questions

After you have finished speaking, there may be an opportunity for questions. A good chairman should ensure that these are real questions, not speeches from the floor of the meeting. Often it is a good idea to take the questions in 'rounds of three' which means three questions are taken in one go from the floor before you stand to answer them. This gives you the advantage of being able to focus on the questions you want to, and play down those you don't.

You might want to consider 'planting' some questions covering areas that you want to speak on. This gives you the opportunity to make the points that you want to, and also makes less time available for your opponents to ask questions that you are less happy to tackle. If you can guarantee some planted questions, you can prepare good 'set-piece' answers, and it allows you to cover other areas in your main remarks, secure in the knowledge you will get the chance during questions to make the points that you want. Be careful not to plant too many questions, because the audience will be suspicious. Some political meetings have more dodgy plants than a Tory front-bencher's greenhouse.

You should ask the chairman to request that all contributors should state their name and where they've come from. You should make a note of the questioner's name, and use it in your answer. The personal touch is the mark of a good speaker. Courtesy also goes a long way. At the end of questions, you may be given the chance to 'sum up'. Here, you have the opportunity to thank the audience for the quality of the questions and contributions and thank people for coming along to the meeting.

Top tips for speaking in public

1 Always prepare – no one can speak 'off the cuff'
2 Time in reconnaissance is never wasted – check out the room and set-up
3 Judge the audience, and speak accordingly
4 Use props or visual aids
5 Think about your appearance and body langage
6 Use the microphone, lectern and table to your advantage
7 Use jokes, imagery, rhetorical devices – anything to make it more interesting
8 Take questions, and treat questioners with respect no matter how difficult
9 Be polite at all times, and never let your annoyance show.

5   Indirect Campaigning I: The Media

Direct forms of communication are highly effective, but no matter how many meetings you speak at and doors you knock on you cannot reach enough people without recourse to indirect campaigning via the media, advertising, printed materials and the Internet.

The role of the media

When Prime Minister Clement Attlee was stopped by waiting journalists outside Downing Street at the start of the 1950 general election, he was asked if he would like to make a comment on the forthcoming campaign. He replied: 'no'. Indeed, until the mid-nineteen fifties, the media were banned from discussing any matter due to be debated in the Commons or Lords for fourteen days beforehand. Winston Churchill believed 'it would be shocking to have debates in this House forestalled, time after time, by expressions of opinion by persons who had not the status or responsibility of MPs.' Things have changed somewhat since then.

The media matters in an election campaign. National campaigns are fought out in the media – through the pages of newspapers, and on radio and TV programmes. Much of your election campaign should revolve around ways of getting into the media – because it is in the media that the campaign will be largely fought out. The media is one of the main channels of communication with your target voters. You will never meet more than a few hundred local voters, even if you knock on doors all day for a year. A single appearance on a local radio station can reach tens of thousands of your potential supporters in under five minutes.

Every week in Britain, 200 million newspapers are bought. There are 21 national newspapers, 89 regional dailies, and 1500 local weekly titles. The British buy three times as many newspapers as the French. And for every paper sold, more than one person will end up reading it, as copies are left on the bus and around the kitchen table. By the same token, millions watch national and regional television and listen to national and local radio. The media remains most people's main source of news and views every day.

In the media, your image in the minds of the voters will be built up and sustained. Despite the healthy cynicism of most people, the media helps create that which we accept as the truth and reality of the world around us. If they see you week after week active in pursuit of laudable aims, they will develop a sympathy with you, even if they disagree with your policies. Voters prefer an active candidate they see doing things than one they don't, regardless of party affiliations.

Every aspect of your campaign should include a media angle. Out campaigning? Take a few photos for the local paper. Meeting local nurses? Invite the local journalists along for the ride. No campaign can afford to ignore the media.

The impact of the media on election results

Many in the media like to think that the coverage and analysis of politics has a major impact on election results. The partisan tabloid newspapers extol the virtues of their chosen party and the dangers of the other lot, often in ways of which Goebbels would have been proud. The switch of the *Sun* from supporting the Conservatives to supporting Labour in 1997 was seen as a huge boost for Tony Blair's campaign, and a kick in the teeth for the Tories. In 1992, after a lacklustre Conservative campaign, the *Sun* boasted 'it was the Sun wot won it' for the Tories. The vicious and unfair pounding that the *Sun* gave Neil Kinnock, with 14 pages of 'Nightmare on Kinnock Street' and the polling day headline asking for the last person to leave Britain to turn off the lights if Labour won, must have had an influence on some people as they went to vote.

But the case that the media influences votes can be overstated. Only the newspapers can be overtly biased. The broadcast media is regulated and must maintain fair coverage, both in terms of length given to party leaders and balance given to issues. Even the role of the partisan newspapers is marginal to the result. Did the *Sun's* decision to back Labour in

1997 make a difference to the result, or did *Sun* executives know that their readers were switching to Labour and they knew they must reflect their own readership? Do the tabloids lead or follow the national mood? Voting behaviour is determined by a range of complex factors, especially personal economics and general impressions about politics, rather than simply what a tabloid newspaper says you should do.

Messages for the media

Politics can be a complex business. The real nitty-gritty of politics can be about tax rates, changes to the benefit system, legalistic directives from Europe, scientific issues like new variant CJD or genetic modification of crops, constitutional issues like different election systems, and a range of other areas where politicians make decisions about areas they may know little about in detail.

But the people on whose behalf those decisions are being taken have no interest in the detail. They have no time to listen to convoluted arguments or to read lengthy policy documents. People's daily lives are filled with a cacophony of noise from a million and one sources – retailers, manufacturers, banks, movie-makers, all trying to sell their wares. The bustle and noise of the bazaar is brought into our homes every morning when we turn on the television, listen to the radio, pick up a paper, log on to the Internet. Once we leave our homes, stepping over the mountain of unsolicited direct mail, we are bombarded with messages on hoardings, on the sides of buses, in our daily newspapers.

At work we are subjected to 'word of mouth' – people repeating information and views they have heard over the past 24 hours. We switch on our computers, and advertisers are reaching us via the Internet and email. In amongst all these frantic attempts to attract our attention is politics. The candidate in an election is like a man holding up a sign in the midst of a Cup Final crowd – insignificant and likely to be missed.

The breakdown of strong party loyalty, with voters behaving more like consumers in their voting habits, means that people can pick and choose which bits of politics they agree with. People are voting less tribally, no longer following either the reds or the blues as they might follow the local football teams, and are starting to discern from election to election. They may vote one way at one election, and differently the next. When presented with the opportunity to vote at a national and a local level on the same day, they may vote for one party to run the country and for another to run the council. Places like Wandsworth have a Labour MP but a Conservative Council.

People are less motivated by issues, especially the detail of issues, and more stirred by impressions. Impressions are what increasingly count in politics. The Tories raised taxes when they were in office, but they created the impression, through constant repetition of their messages, that they were the tax-cutting party. Labour in 1992 laid out their detailed tax plans in a Government-style 'Red Book' – but people had the impression that their tax plans really went much further, largely thanks to the Conservatives election campaign. Impressions matter in politics.

The majority of people have little time to think about politics. They know very little about the issues, and they are not very interested. People are busy doing other things – working, socialising, and surviving.

That's why politics must be packaged. It must be presented. It must succumb, whether we like it or not, to the adman's and PR man's expertise. Politics is too important to leave to the politicians and *cognoscenti*. Everyone must get a chance to hear the debate and form a view. One of the main skills for the candidate is therefore the ability to communicate politics in a way people can relate to, swiftly digest, and form an understanding. This means that political communications must be professionalised. We in this country are a long way from the professionalisation which characterises American politics, where political campaign consultants sell their skills to the highest bidder, but we have seen the rise of the campaign professional and modern techniques within the party apparatus.

The modern politician is a prisoner of this world of instant information and packaging. Tony Blair, in every sense a modern politician, has said 'Our news today is instant, hostile to subtlety or qualification. If you can't sum it up in a sentence or even a phrase, forget it.'

It has been argued that this means that politics is being 'dumbed-down' – that issues are trivialised and debates polarised to cope with an ever restless, channel-hopping, consumer society where attention-spans are shrinking. The culture of 'soundbites' has been condemned because it is felt that the people are being treated like idiots by politicians.

Is soundbite culture reducing politics to the level of the lowest common denominator? The ability to package politics, to present arguments in digestible chunks, and to communicate with a disinterested populace has always been part of the politician's art. When Lenin wanted to rouse the Russian masses to revolution in 1917, he didn't hand out volumes of *State and Revolution* or *Das Kapital*. He wrote pamphlets and made speeches that people would understand. He distilled his revolutionary theory into a single soundbite which summed up the Bolshevik demands: 'Bread, Peace, Land.' This soundbite is memorable and concise, and speaks directly to individuals' desires. It is not an appeal to altruism, but an appeal to self-interest. It also encompasses the coalition of forces whose support Lenin needed. The urban proletariat wanted the bread, the army and navy wanted peace, the agricultural workers wanted land. All that, in just three words.

One reason the fuel blockaders, who wanted a multi-billion pound cut in fuel prices, lost public support in late 2000 was because of the inarticulacy of their spokespeople. The self-appointed leaders of the protestors would appear on radio and television opposite professional politicians and interviewers, and appear mumbling, confused, and thick. Their views were ill-formed and poorly expressed. They had no clear, single campaign objective. They contradicted and publicly argued with each other. And in the end they crumbled in the face of media scrutiny, and were outgunned by the Government's star media performers like Gus MacDonald.

Soundbites are a product of the modern broadcast media. The need to sandwich politics in between news of floods, famines, earthquakes and wars, celebrity marriages, sports results, business news and the weather, means that there is little space for politicians to develop arguments or elucidate their positions on matters of the day. Politicians must say what they mean in a few seconds, in a way which makes sense, and which people can remember. Soundbites are shrinking in size. In the late 1960s, politicians could expect 40 seconds. This had halved by the 1980s, and by the 1992 general election even the party leaders could expect 22 seconds on the BBC *Nine O'Clock News* and 16 seconds on the ITV *News at Ten*. During the 1997 general election, soundbites were on average 16.5 seconds in duration on the BBC *Nine O'Clock News* and 14.7 seconds on the ITV *News at Ten*. The growth of video and sound clips used by news outlets on the Internet, where users can click on an icon to hear a politician's soundbite, will only exacerbate the problem.

Soundbite culture leaves little time for wasted words. Every one must count.

Soundbites are used as part of speeches. Within a half-hour speech, the politician will try to include a phrase which sums up the point of the speech or illuminates a particular point. At conferences and big set-piece speeches, the spin doctor will often have a copy of the speech in advance with the soundbites marked in the text, to show to journalists what the memorable phrases will be. Broadcasters will be tipped off that a particular section of the speech is the one to record and broadcast. In the past, when this practice was not observed, the media might miss an important part of a speech. Film of Enoch Powell's notorious 'rivers of blood' speech exists, but not the part when he actually refers to 'the Tiber foaming with much blood' because the camera crew failed to have the camera on for that section of the speech.

The following political soundbites were all made on public platforms, often during election campaigns:

- 'What is our task? To make Britain a fit country for heroes to live in' (Lloyd George)
- 'U-turn if you want to; the Lady's not for turning' (Margaret Thatcher)
- 'Most of our people have never had it so good' (Harold Macmillan)
- 'The wind of change is blowing through this continent' (Harold Macmillan)
- 'An iron curtain has descended across Europe' (Winston Churchill)
- 'Like the Roman, I seem to see "the River Tiber foaming with much blood"' (Enoch Powell)
- 'Time to get back to basics' (John Major)
- 'Tough on crime, tough on the causes of crime' (Tony Blair).

Some, such as 'winds of change' and 'iron curtain' have entered popular discourse. Sometimes the soundbite that is reported or remembered from the speech was never actually uttered by the politician. Lloyd George never said 'a land fit for heroes', Powell never said 'rivers of blood', Norman Tebbit never said 'on your bike' and James Callaghan never said 'crisis, what crisis?' A journalist in each case has reported the speech using their own shorthand version of what was said, or in the case of 'crisis, what crisis' or 'on your bike', the headline writers have written what they thought the politician should have said.

Some soundbites do not emanate from a politician's mouth at all. The phrase 'Winter of Discontent' used to describe the industrial unrest in winter 1978 was thrown at Labour for twenty years. It was one of the most effective jibes for Conservatives to use. It was coined not by a politician, but by Larry Lamb, the editor of the *Sun*. Others come back to haunt the soundbiter –a case of the biter bit. George Bush Snr. rued the day he said 'Watch my lips, no new taxes' and John Major wished he'd never extolled the virtues of going 'back to basics'.

Today, the political battlefield rings to the noise of soundbites fired by one party against another, each hoping their soundbite will find a target. The Tories talk of 'Tony's cronies'. Their European policy is 'In Europe but not run by Europe'. Their economics is based on the 'tax guarantee'. Labour's response is that they have 'lurched to the right', and that Labour deserves a second term because there's 'a lot done, a lot still to do.'

In 2000 Tony Blair coined a bizarre soundbite in his conference speech when he talked about his 'irreducible core' of beliefs. My favourite contemporary soundbite is the soundbite which denied it was a soundbite, delivered with more than a pinch of chutzpah by Tony Blair at the signing of the Northern Ireland Good Friday Agreement: 'Now is not the time for soundbites. I feel the hand of history on my shoulder.'

Creating your messages

So how should you construct your own soundbites?

You should think about the essential, core message that you want to get across. If you had to encapsulate your message into a single sentence – what would it be? Remember your audience will not know much about the issue, so avoid any technical language or jargon. You are talking to the broadcast audience, the people watching television at home or listening to the radio in their cars, not the interviewer or fellow interviewees, so keep things simple and direct.

Use active, lively, punchy words and phrases. You should think about alliterative phrases, where the words start with the same letter, such as 'back to basics' or 'building a better Britain'. Your soundbite might contain a rhyme such as 'Tony's cronies'. It could use the same phrasing twice, with a twist on the second phrase: 'Tough on crime, tough on the causes of crime' or 'In Europe, but not run by Europe'. You could try humour, such as Churchill's 'some chicken, some neck' speech, or Michael Heseltine's 'never have so many crustaceans died in vain' referring to Labour's prawn cocktail offensive on businessmen and the City. Imagery (without straying too far into the realms of cliché) can be effective.

Practice your soundbite out loud to get your mouth around the words. What looks good on paper, or sounds good in your head, might be better expressed out loud. Practise the phrase over and over again, and hone it down. A good soundbite will live on in the public imagination, be repeated and referred to during the course of political discussion, and perhaps even be immortalised in one of the dictionaries of quotations.

Dealing with journalists

You've decided what you want to say, and tested out your messages. You've practiced your soundbites. Now it is time to start dealing with the media.

Who are journalists?

There are tens of thousands of journalists working in Britain today, in all branches of the media – local, national, print, broadcast, Internet, news, features, freelance – so to attempt to characterise journalists as a single social group is a risky endeavour. But there are common features of what makes a journalist tick, what appeals, and what turns them off.

The basic job titles and roles of journalists are:

Reporter

The reporter's job is to research and write stories for newspapers or radio and television. They are at the sharp end of the process, and for candidates in elections, represent the type of journalist most likely to be dealt with. They want news, because without news they cannot do their jobs, and they are slaves to the deadline so do not waste their time. They deal with every subject under the sun – one minute it could be drug trafficking, the next it could be Posh and Becks. If dealing with a reporter, you should take time to spell things out and explain your story from first principles. This is not because they are stupid, but because they deal with such a wide range of subjects they may not be fully familiar with the detail and nuance of political campaigning.

Specialist correspondent

Some journalists develop a specialist area or subject and cover stories in that field for national news outlets or for specialist magazines or programmes. Political specialists tend to work at Westminster, but many of the political commentators may work at the news headquarters, or even as freelances at home. Specialists may cover areas such as health, education, law, football, show business, the City, local government, and a range of other areas. Specialist correspondents develop excellent contacts with other players in the field, on the conference and rubber chicken circuit, and often become acknowledged experts in their areas. This means that unlike general reporters who know a little about a lot, specialists know a lot, and probably more than you, about their chosen field.

Freelance

Unlike the reporter and specialist correspondent, the freelance does not work on the staff of a newspaper or broadcaster, but instead works by selling their talents to whichever media outlet wants them. Most freelances have regular work from a small number of newspapers, magazines or broadcasters, but are always on the look out for new stories and new sources of income. Freelances may be fairly new to journalism. Sometimes freelancing is a euphemism for unemployment; sometimes the term doesn't do justice to the established authors, writers and commentators who earn their living by writing and contributing to the media without working for a single employer.

News Editor

The News Editor is the person to whom reporters are accountable and who take the decisions about which stories will appear and which won't. Candidates won't have regular contact with news editors, but they are worth getting to know for two reasons: first, if the reporter knows you have a good relationship with their boss they will be more likely to treat you fairly, and second, if the reporter doesn't treat you fairly or if you are misrepresented, it is the news editor you should complain to in the first instance.

Editor

Local candidates should get to know their local newspaper editors, not in order to try to place stories, but because they are influential opinion-formers in a local constituency. They should be cultivated in the same way local business leaders, community leaders or religious leaders should be. At the national level, politicians at the most senior levels spend time talking to newspaper editors and the editors of programmes such as *Today* or *Newsnight* because of their influence over the way political parties are covered. Margaret Thatcher recalls in *The Path to Power* that 'whatever the other demands on my diary, when Gordon (Reece – her spin doctor) said that we must have lunch with such-and-such an editor, that was the priority.'

Producer

On radio and television, the producer serves in the same capacity as news editor. They decide what goes on and what does not. They are the person to whom complaints should be addressed. Like editors, they should be cultivated.

Researcher/Production Assistant

The first person to contact you from a broadcasting outfit will probably be a junior member of staff called a researcher or production assistant. Their job is to contact possible contributors to the programme and sound them out. They may ask for your views on a subject and see whether they are interesting or trenchant enough to merit your inclusion in the programme. Like those doing so many other jobs at the bottom of organisations, the researchers and production assistants are worth being pleasant and helpful to, because today's researchers are tomorrow's producers and presenters, and they will remember if you treated them poorly.

Political staff

On a national newspaper or major broadcaster the political correspondents are established figures in their own right. The senior correspondents are often better known to the British public than the politicians they interview. The lower ranks are filled with intelligent, Oxbridge-educated young men and women. Those journalists sent to Parliament to cover politics join the 'Lobby' which is the elite band of journalists licensed to work inside the Palace of Westminster, with crammed offices off the Press Gallery, and more importantly, access to the Members' Lobby. This Lobby, between the Central Lobby where the public is allowed, and the Chamber of the House of Commons, is where only MPs, Commons staff, and members of the Lobby are allowed, and it is here that political gossip and news is incubated, disseminated, and enhanced in the telling.

Local journalists

On a local newspaper, the journalists tend to fall into one of two camps. Either they are early-twenties, fresh from being qualified as a journalist, on their first or second job, keen to make a name for themselves, and ambitious for a job on a national title. They are keen to build a portfolio of clippings of hard-hitting stories they've written to show to prospective employers, and know they are just passing through the local paper on the way to Fleet Street. This makes them dangerous because they will not be interested in developing long-term relationships with local sources, including candidates, and will not be above going for the sensationalist angle for the sake of a by-line on the front page.

The second kind is the older, seasoned, veteran of the local paper. They've worked the patch for decades, know everyone and everything, and have forgotten more about the area than most people will ever know. Some are content in their role, love their area and its people, and do an excellent job. Others are frustrated by their lack of advancement, bitter that they never quite 'made it', and held back by a lack of talent or love of the bottle.

On local radio, particularly the BBC, the staff tend to be those earning their spurs before graduating to national radio.

Contacts

'Contacts' are the journalists you come across during your campaigning and other activity. A journalist has a contact book, which contains the names and numbers of a range of people who can act as sources of information. Many contacts will go back years, even decades. The contacts book is one of the journalists' most valuable assets, because the accumulated information is irreplaceable, and is the result of years of journalism.

Candidates need to cultivate their own contacts. Every constituency has a handful of local journalists working on the local papers. At the regional level there is radio and television. There are also national political journalists and the researchers on regional and national political discussion programmes. Every time you have contact with a journalist, you should make a note of their name and number, and keep the contact alive. This should not be by adding them to your fax database for news releases, so that they are inundated with news releases which may be entirely irrelevant to them. Local journalists should be contacted regularly in person, and invited for a drink every few months leading up to election day. You should be ready to give them titbits of information and gossip every now and again to keep them interested. 'All-points' news releases should be supported by the use of exclusives and leaks to make the journalist feel special. Even those journalists with whom you seldom have contact should be kept aware of your campaign with the occasional phone-call or note, or even just a Christmas card.

All politicians cultivate their own contacts in the media. Some know journalists over many decades and build up a relationship based on trust. The politician can rely on fair or even favourable coverage; the journalist can rely on a regular supply of inside information and exclusive stories. As both politician and journalist progress through their careers, the contact is kept going, so that a politician who starts off as the leader of the local council and ends up in the Cabinet is still talking to the journalist who started off on the local weekly and ended up in the Lobby.

You must ensure that your contact details are kept up to date. Journalism has a very rapid turnover of staff, especially on local newspapers. There will be new journalists starting work every year in your area, and each one is worth contacting and getting to know.

The reason for this spadework is that during the election campaign itself, things may move very quickly and you will need to be able to deal with journalists on a speedy basis. There will be no time for 'getting to know you' small-talk. The other reason is that if a journalist knows you personally, and has enjoyed your company and hospitality, it is harder for them to write up a story attacking you. A few drinks won't make a journalist forget they are a journalist, and ignore a dynamite story about you, even if it is damaging to your campaign. But a personal relationship, built over time, will make a journalist err on the side of caution, and even in the worst case scenario, give you a decent right to reply. Some journalists, in their lust for headlines, will do you over no matter what, which can be an added blow to a politician who thought they were his or her friend. The rule is: you can be friendly with journalists, but they are never your friends.

Deadlines

Journalists' lives revolve around deadlines. A deadline is the time by which the journalist must have completed and submitted their news article or sound package for inclusion in the newspaper or bulletin. Most people at work can put off until this afternoon what they cannot do this morning. If you've got a hangover, you can cruise until the coffee has properly kicked in, and do your work when you're feeling fresher.

For a journalist, the option doesn't exist. Deadlines are non-negotiable, immoveable, and to miss them is to risk the sack. When dealing with journalists, it is important to know when the deadlines fall, and when you need to get your information to the journalist in time for them to use your material.

A conversation when a journalist is nearing a deadline will be fraught, abrupt and possibly cut short. If you phone them with hours to go before a deadline, they will have more time and be more relaxed. If you phone a local radio station just before the hour, everyone will be working towards the news bulletin at the top of the hour, and will have no time for you. If you phone at ten past the hour, the news will have been and gone, and the journalists will be more receptive. A quarter of an hour can make all the difference.

When phoning a journalist, you should do them the courtesy of asking if it is a convenient time to talk, and if not, find out when is a better time.

Knowing when newspaper deadlines are, especially on the local weekly titles that candidates deal with most, will also inform your decisions about when to issue news releases, hold photo-opportunities, or send in letters. If you miss the deadline, your time has been wasted.

Tools of the trade

There are various ways to attract journalists' attention and start to influence the way the media covers your campaign activities and your message. They include news releases, photo-opportunities, doing radio and television interviews, writing letters and articles, and getting quoted in the newspapers. The key to successful media relations is to use every tool in the toolkit. Your campaign should utilise a range of different methods of dealing with the media, from the personal phone-call, to letter-writing, to the traditional news release.

At the heart of your campaign must be the concept of giving journalists what they want and what they can use to do their jobs. The most important aspect of this approach is dealing in 'news.' If you can create news, then journalists will give you the column inches and airtime that you need to reach the voters.

Creating news

The news agency Reuters said that news is 'fires, explosions, floods ... railway accidents, destructive storms, earthquakes, shipwrecks ... accidents ... street riots ... strikes ... the suicide of people of note, social or political, and murders of a sensational or atrocious character.' And that was in 1883!

News is more than something new. Newness is the starting point, but not the end of the story. You should be telling journalists what is about to happen, not what happened last week. But journalists are trained to look for news which also contains one or more of the following characteristics:

- Conflict
- Unusualness

- Danger
- Celebrity
- Scandal
- Success/Failure.

If you open today's newspaper, you will see stories which reflect these 'news values'.

Few political stories can be written without reference to conflict. Politics and sport are usually discussed as though they were war. But the confrontation of politics, between competing political parties and their leaders is what people expect, so journalists are on the look out for other forms of conflict. A candidate can receive far more coverage if they attack the leader of their own party instead of the leader of their opposition. Splits and divisions make for interesting news stories. So stories about Michael Portillo leaving the Thatcherite 'No Turning Back' group, or Peter Kilfoyle attacking Tony Blair for 'ignoring the heartlands' receive more attention than opponents attacking each other.

'Unusualness' covers a variety of stories from the lurid (tallest ever man, eleven-year old with maths degree) to the amusing (dogs that can talk). 'Danger' usually means a threat to a community, for example from flooding, from job losses, or from a new disease. 'Celebrity' is one of the drivers of the modern media, with new celebrities being invented all the time. 'Scandal' is well known to the world of politics, and to be avoided if possible. And 'success or failure' covers attempts to reach the North Pole by balloon, cross the Atlantic in a bath, or beat some record or other. In political terms, 'success' is sought from claiming success in an international round of negotiations, for example when Tony Blair returned from the Nice summit in December 2000, or success in a by-election (even if their party didn't actually win).

News stories are always about people. People are what make stories real and relevant. A journalist will seldom cover a story without reference to the people affected, and interviews and photographs of them. The terrible flooding in Britain in late-2000 was covered by the media as a national story, but made up of a thousand and one individual stories of tragedy. As editor and journalist Harold Evans has said: 'news is about people; it is people doing and people talking'. Politics is only about people; what politicians do has an effect on everyone's lives. So when communicating with the electorate through the media, you should always tell your story by using people – real examples, real testimonies, real lives.

In the world of the local media, the most important criterion is whether the story is local. A local newspaper or regional radio or television station can only cover a story 'on their patch' and won't touch a story, no matter how newsworthy, in another area.

Writing news releases

'I keep these honest serving men
They taught me all I knew
Their names are What and Why and When
And How and Where and Who.'

Rudyard Kipling

All over the country, indeed the world, hopeful candidates are devising news releases for their local media, the overwhelming majority of which end up in the waste bin. The reason why most news releases have the same survival rate as lemmings once they've been sent is because the originator has failed to understand what a news release is for. A news release has a simple purpose – to attract sufficient attention and interest from a journalist to persuade them to want to find out more, and to cover your story in his or her newspaper or bulletin. That's it. A successful news release is one which provokes a journalist to action. An unsuccessful news release is one which fails to stir them.

News releases are the basic, but not the only, tool of dealing with the media. They form the standard interface between a journalist and a candidate during a campaign. Once they were posted, then they were faxed, now they can be emailed. They can be sent by email with photographs and documents attached. But unless they are well-written and contain newsworthy material, they will fail.

So many news releases fail because the writer does not understand one or more of the basic rules of writing a news release, they produce it in the wrong format, or target it at the wrong person. The more random elements that are introduced to the process, the less likely the chances of success.

You should keep up a regular flow of news releases to your local media, but don't let quality be sacrificed for frequency. It is better to have one good story in the local weekly every other week than try to get one in every week and fail. Don't be afraid to offer exclusives on stories and give preferential treatment to different media, as long as you spread your favours around. An exclusive is far more likely to be covered than something which is spread around all the local journalists.

So how do you write a successful news release?
The best way is to practise and see what works and what doesn't, but the theory runs like this.

The first stage is to be clear what you want to happen. You want to provoke a journalist to do something. Here the advertising formula AIDA is helpful. Your news release should provoke from the target journalist:

- Attention
- Interest
- Desire
- Action

Unlike advertisers, the desire you are provoking is a desire to know more rather than to buy the product, and the action required is to start thinking about how to write a story rather than to go out shopping for the product, but the basic cognitive process is identical.

We are fortunate in this country to have professional qualifications for . Most of the journalists you meet will hold a National Council for the Training of Journalists (NCTJ) qualification, or an equivalent qualification. Some will have degrees or Masters in Journalism from one of the main centres of training: Cardiff, London, or Sheffield. Most journalists will have been taught in similar ways using similar textbooks how to do their jobs, and this means that if you can understand how they have been trained, you can tailor your information to attract their attention.

Sometimes you will be supplying feature material, or letters, or photographs. Most of the time, you should be supplying journalists with news. Your news release is a way of convincing a journalist that your story is news. And remember that even a journalist on a small circulation weekly paper receives hundreds of news releases every week. Yours is just part of a big pile of paper and faxes.

News release format
News releases should follow a particular format to guide the journalist through the information in a speedy and efficient fashion. Your format should be designed to help the journalist scan over the release and become interested in a matter of seconds.

News releases should be double-spaced, to allow sub-editors to scribble their editing marks, and single sided so that the journalists do not have to turn it over. They should never be longer than two sides. At the top goes the place the release is from, for example 'NEWS FROM LABOUR' or 'LIBERAL DEMOCRAT NEWS' and the phrase 'News Release' so that the reader is in no doubt what he or she is holding.

It should contain, in order:

- Organisation name and logo
- The words 'NEWS RELEASE' or 'NEWS FROM LABOUR' etc
- The date or an embargo
- 24-hour contact details
- Headline
- First paragraph, with the guts of the story
- Two or three more paragraphs
- A Quote
- 'more follows' if it goes onto a second page
- The word 'ends' at the end
- 24-hour contact details again
- Notes to editors

Date or embargo?

Because news journalists deal in news, they want to know how newsworthy your information is. If it happened last week, forget it. You can either put today's date on your release preceded by the words 'For immediate release' or place the information under an embargo. 'For immediate release' means that the information in the release can be published or broadcast with immediate effect. An embargo means that the journalist is required to not publish or broadcast the information to the public until the time you stipulate. An embargo does not mean that the journalist cannot start working on the story, making phone-calls, or asking others for comment.

An embargo might be used when you are making a speech to a constituency meeting. You can alert the journalist to the event in advance and let them know what you intend to say. Often information about the text of speeches is also marked 'Check against delivery' which means that the journalist should check that you said in your speech what you said you would.

Mostly, this convention works to the benefit of all sides, but not always. The news release containing the main points of Tony Blair's speech to the Women's Institute did not reveal what would actually happen in the event, when some of the speech was scrapped because of the hostile reaction of some of the audience.

24-Hour contact details

The numbers you give on the release must be the numbers you are available on. Because of the tyranny of deadlines, if a journalist phones the number on your release they need to speak to you right away. If they cannot get through because the number is an evenings-only, or on an answerphone, or you've gone on holiday, they may drop your story altogether and start work on something else. Candidates should use mobile phones and possibly also pagers so that journalists can always reach them. Those politicians you always see on television and hear on radio or see quoted in the press may not always have the most interesting point to make, but they are the most available.

Headline

You headline should be short, snappy and informative, but do not try to win any awards. The job of a headline on a news release is to attract interest in the story, but you do not need to spend hours thinking up *Sun*-style puns and alliteration – that's the job of the journalists. Headlines should not be too long – no more than two lines ('a double-decker'). Try to get the main thrust of the story into the headline, for example:

'Tory candidate slams cuts in police numbers'
'Labour praises drop in class sizes'
'Government has failed on environment, say Liberal Democrats'

First paragraph

In the first paragraph (or 'par' as journalists say), the battle is won or lost. If you can hook in a journalist with your first paragraph, the chances are that they will cover your story and invest time in writing it up.

The best training for writing crisp, snappy first paragraphs is to practise over and over again. Look at the opening paragraphs of newspaper stories, especially the tabloids. Take your style from the *Mirror* and *Sun*. See the economy of language and the use of short, powerful words. Expressing information in a short paragraph with only 20-odd words is far harder than writing 200.

The first par contains the guts of the story, laid out for all to see. The traditional formula for an opening paragraph is the Five 'W's:

- Who?
- What?
- Where?
- Why ?
- When?

Answering these questions gives you the nuts and bolts of the story. The real skill, in both news release writing and journalism, is to decide which 'W' is the most interesting. Choosing which 'W' to start with – whether it is who, what, where, why, or when – gives you the angle for the story. Most of us hope that the 'who' is the most interesting part, so most candidates' news release start with 'Joe Bloggs, Conservative candidate for Oxford South, said today ... ' But to a journalist, the 'who' may not be the most interesting angle. Don't always start with yourself when you are writing a news release, you will soon turn the journalist off, and it may end up in the bin without being read. When crafting your opening sentence, you should imagine yourself in the shoes of the journalist reading your release, and what their reactions might be.

On a local paper or radio station, the 'where' is the most important 'W' because if it is off their patch, they will not be interested. If you are doing some kind of stunt such as a parachute jump or a wacky photo-opportunity, the 'what' is the most interesting angle.

In subsequent paragraphs you can fill in some of the details and end with a pithy quote. Be sure not to 'bury' nuggets of information down the page, because the reader might not even get that far.

You need to spell it out to the journalist with the word 'ends' if the text has come to an end, but if your news release goes onto a second page, you should write 'more follows' to steer the journalist onto the next page. News releases are never double-sided.

The Notes to Editors at the end contains the standard phrase which explains who you are and what you stand for. A second note to editor might include technical information such as a photograph being available or some background to the story.

You can fax, post or email your news release – perhaps all three to make sure – as long as you do it with enough time before the journalists' deadline for them to work on the story. In your campaign office you should build up a file of news releases, with index numbers, so that you can refer swiftly to anything and everything you've said during your candidacy. This is useful in order to rebut an opponent who is challenging you, it allows a campaign volunteer to be able to find out the 'line' on an issue without having to ask you, and it allows your position on hot issues to be clear for enquiries from voters.

News release content

What kinds of news stories should your news releases cover? Again, you should suck it and see. Some journalists like particular types of stories, and won't cover others. You could do worse than to buy the journalist lunch and ask them what stories they like. Most campaigns will consist of the following categories of story:

Introduce your candidate

Your campaign has to start somewhere. Announce the selection of your candidate to the constituency. Say how he or she was selected and from how many contenders (this is to make the position seem hotly contested and valued). Include some biographical details such as their job, local history if any, and some colour such as if they have children, what they do for fun, what teams they support. Offer an interview with the candidate and have some photographs ready. You may also want to include an endorsement from a respected local figure.

Demands for action from the Council/Government
There are plenty of things that local people want doing. Your role as candidate is to articulate those demands and present yourself as a tribune of the people even before taking up office. The Liberal Democrats are very good at using news releases to demand local action, say the filling in of a pothole, when they know that the council is planning to do the work anyway. When the action takes place, the Lib Dems take the credit and reinforce their campaigning credentials.

Praise for government action, with a local twist
If your side are in office locally or nationally, there is a wealth of policy initiatives which have an effect locally, from spending on schools, initiatives for business, health reforms, or whatever it might be. Take the national picture and see how it relates to your own area. If the policy is popular, find some local people who have benefited from it and ask them to be used in your news release. If you can tell the story through real people and their lives, it is preferable to dry statistics and raw data.

Demands for your opponent to act/state their views on an issue
Try and paint your opponent into a corner by asking them to come out on an issue which is difficult for them, or to do something they don't want to. Many politicians want to tread a delicate line on issues which divide their party locally or nationally, such as Europe, or air traffic control part-privatisation, and may not want to have to state a clear view one way or the other. They don't want you to force their hand.

Challenges to your opponent for a debate
If you are the challenger in a seat, challenge the incumbent to a debate. If they say yes, you are placed on a par with them and have the chance for voters to make direct comparisons; if they refuse, you can accuse them of being chicken. You can run this challenge throughout the campaign. If you

News from the Liberal Democrats

LIBERAL DEMOCRATS

For immediate release: 4th April 2001
Contact: Fred Sandal, Liberal Democrats' Press Officer
XXX XXX XXX
or mobile XXXXXXX or pager XXXXXXXXX

KIDS IN DANGER: LIB DEMS DEMAND PARK CLEAN-UP

Local children are in danger from broken bottles, rusty cans and even hypodermic needles in the play area Anytown Park, and Joan Candidate, Lib Dem parliamentary spokesperson for Anytown is demanding that the park is cleaned up. The campaigner has written to John Tammany-Hall, leader of the council and local MP Sarah Marginal demanding action to clean up the park.

The park is used by drug addicts and street drinkers after dark, and each morning the play area is littered with dangerous objects. Local children are in danger of injury and infection. In a *Liberal Democrat Focus* survey of the surrounding houses, the dirty and dangerous state of the park was mentioned by 76 per cent of residents as a priority for action.

Joan Candidate said: *'the park is a disgrace and the council are to blame. They've done nothing to clean up their act. Our local amenities are becoming shabby and dangerous. The Lib Dems demand action.'*

Joan Candidate is available for a photo-opportunity in Anytown Park with examples of the dangerous material which mars the play area, and meeting local parents.

ends

Notes to editors:
1) Joan Candidate is the Liberal Democrat parliamentary spokesperson for Anytown constituency which includes the villages of Wooltown, Bridgeford and Cowpass. She is chairwoman of the local Amnesty International branch and works as an economist for the Regional Development Agency.

Sample news release

are holding a public meeting, put out an empty chair on the platform with your opponent's name on it. You can even hire a chicken suit and get a volunteer to follow your opponent round the constituency.

Endorsements

If you can persuade local business or community leaders with good name recognition locally to come out and support you, you can news release their endorsement to the media. 'Third party' endorsements from respected figures are highly influential, because people are more likely to believe independent voices than partisan ones, who 'would say that, wouldn't they?'

Surveys

Surveys can be conducted by local parties to engage people in the high street as part of visibility campaigning, or as a way of creating a news story. Some surveys, if conducted subtly, can be used to help the member of the public reach certain conclusions, This is called 'push polling', and questions might be 'Do you agree with the Government's policy to break up the United Kingdom and pass more power to Brussels – yes or no?' or from the other side 'Do you agree with William Hague's policy of £24 million worth of cuts in public services like education and health in this constituency – yes or no?'

If 80 per cent of OAPs disagree with your opponent's policy on pensions, you have a great story for the local paper. If you can show that your local standing is improving in local opinion polls asking for voting intention, you can create a sense of momentum. In Enfield Southgate, the *Observer* newspaper poll showing that Labour could beat Michael Portillo if people voted tactically for Labour gave the campaign a huge boost the weekend before polling day.

Campaign visits

If your party leaders or celebrities are visiting your constituency, or even a neighbouring constituency, make sure you have a photo taken with them and ask their press officer for a quote from them about a local issue or an endorsement for your campaign. You can use the photographs in local leaflets and newsletters as well as sending it to the local papers.

Defections

If you can persuade a local member of an opposing camp to join you, use the defection to maximum effect. Tell the media, organise a photo-op with a giant new party membership card, use the defector to attack the party they've just left. High profile defections such as Emma Nicholson's defection from the Tories to the Lib Dems, or Shaun Woodward's defection from Tories to Labour always attract attention and serve as a signal to floating voters that the 'host' party is worth joining.

Rebuttal to your opponents charges

You can use news releases to rebut the claims your opponent is making about you and your record. Getting your rebuttal on paper and out to the media quickly ensures your side of the argument is heard.

Forthcoming events

For most news outlets, there is a forward planning system which allows editors to plan news stories and features in advance, allocate journalists and photographers, and plan programmes and page layouts. If you can have your events programmed into the forward planning system for newspapers, radio or television, your event has a higher chance of being covered.

Media interviews

'I can evade questions without help; what I need is answers.'

John F. Kennedy

Giving a media interview is a piece of political theatre, which follows certain rules of engagement. To give a successful interview, and to be asked to appear again, you need to know what the rules are.

When you are on the phone to the researcher or producer from the programme, you need to establish a number of points about the interview itself. When the researcher or editor phones you from the radio or television programme and bids for you to appear, you must ask a series of questions to have a clear picture of what is being asked of you. When 'fielding the bid' from the broadcaster, you should ask the following questions:

Why you?

On what basis are you being asked? You must be sure that they have the right person, and that they know what you are likely to say. If they are expecting you to say something different to what you want to say, you must find out first. There's a story that in the days of Roy Plomley presenting *Desert Island Discs* on Radio Four, he sat down opposite Frederick Forsyth and began to interview him. When asked about his novels, Frederick Forsyth smiled sheepishly and said 'Oh, I'm not *that* Frederick Forsyth.'

What is the interview about?

Although you won't be told the exact questions, the subject under discussion should be revealed to you beforehand. This gives you time to prepare what you want to say, think about tricky questions, and practise the interview. Established politicians can strike a deal beforehand with the programme's producers that interviews will not cover certain sensitive subjects. When Clare Short stormed out of the Newsroom South East studios in 1996 it was because she had been asked a question about a train strike that she had been promised she wouldn't be asked.

Live or pre-recorded?

You will either be asked to appear live, or they will ask you to pre-record a clip so that they can broadcast it later. Live broadcasting requires a slick, professional performance as there is no second chance to get it right, but some people prefer live broadcasting because it gives the programme editors no chance for editing your remarks. If you are live, of course, you cannot swear or lose your temper.

Pre-recorded interviews give you a little more leeway, but you still try to be word perfect. If you fluff your lines, you can stop and start again, and the programme's editors will use the word perfect version. It has been known for the programme editors to deliberately use the section of interviews where the spokesperson is caught out or stumped for an answer. It happened to a Liberal Democrat spokesman during a by-election, who was asked what difference a Lib Dem victory would actually make. He was totally speechless, and after an embarrassing pause he asked for another go at answering the question. But the programme-makers used the clip anyway, and the hapless Lib Dem was on the first train home.

Studio or location?

Most of the time, you will be asked into the radio or television studio, but on occasion you might be asked to appear at a location. During elections, this might be at a facility such as a school or hospital, or with voters at a leisure centre or old folks' home. Either way, you need a full address and clear instructions about how to get there and how long it will take.

Alone or with others?

You must find out who else is appearing on the programme. It might be that you are being set up for a head-to-head debate with your opponent, or in the studio with an expert on the issue under discussion. If you are uncomfortable with being juxtaposed with the other person, you can refuse to appear. You can seek assurances from the editor or producer. When Michael Heseltine famously stormed out of a television studio it was because he saw that he was due to sit opposite someone he had been promised by the producers would not be appearing.

Audience participation?

Audiences can make things very difficult for candidates. Margaret Thatcher was made to look flustered by the persistent questioning on the sinking of the Belgrano during the Falklands War, from a television audience member in 1983. Neil Kinnock fluffed his answer to a question about electoral reform from an audience member during the 1992 election. Audiences can often come up with questions which candidates and their advisers cannot predict and prepare for. That's why programmes like *Question Time* and *Any Questions* are so popular – because the unpredictability of the questions increases the likelihood of the politicians being caught out.

If you are asked to appear on a programme and you are not sure about the format, you should check if there is an audience participation component. It might be that the local radio station wants you on for an interview, but then opens you up to callers' questions. You must be prepared.

Who is the presenter?

It is a good idea to ascertain the presenter's name. It might be that you've been interviewed by them before, or that you know them to be a supporter, or enemy, of your cause. You can use the presenter's name at the beginning of the interview, to imply familiarity and being a 'player' at the game, but to overuse it risks sounding obsequious and fawning.

Appearance fee?

You should ask if there is an appearance fee. Many programmes offer a small fee for your appearance – usually under fifty pounds – but it is available if you ask. You can keep you fee as long as you declare it, or you can donate it to your local party or charity.

Is travel part of the deal?

Some broadcasters will arrange to have you picked up by car and taken home afterwards from the interview, and if offered, you might want to take advantage of the offer. It can add a moment or two of feeling important to the excitement of being interviewed.

Appearance

If you are appearing uninvited in people's living rooms via their television sets, the least you can do is look smart. Put a suit on, and look professional and business-like. For men that means a shirt and tie; for women a suit and blouse. The days when political candidates could loaf about in woolly jumpers, tee-shirts, open-necked shirts, cardies, and dungarees are over.

You should go for neutral, unfussy colours and patterns, and avoid anything too bright or lively. Go for dark suits, and pale shirts or blouses. Women should avoid distracting brooches or Pat-from-Eastenders earrings. There is one London councillor who often appears on London-wide television being interviewed on serious subjects wearing huge glasses with technicoloured frames. She may be making good points, but all the viewers are registering is the Elton John specs. Men should avoid clunking cuff-links, bracelets or tie-pins. If you are being interviewed at a conference or seminar, remember to take off your name badge or conference credential. If it is sunny, take off your sunglasses – you are a candidate, not a member of U2.

Certain kinds of stripes or close checks on material can cause 'strobing' which means the cameras cannot handle the pattern and the viewers see your jacket or trousers come alive and start dancing around the screen. The same is true of some shades of blue, which are used as the backdrop to project the weather maps or outside broadcasts, and you run the risk of your torso becoming a map of the UK with clouds and suns.

At certain times of the year, you should be aware of the various charity campaigns which involve a lapel badge of some kind. From 1 November, no candidate or politician should be seen on television without a Royal Legion poppy; you might choose your appearance to promote another cause by wearing a badge – for example the AIDS awareness red ribbon or the breast cancer pink ribbon, or the NSPCC's green 'Full Stop' badge.

If you are being interviewed on a sofa, be careful to pull your socks up so that there is no exposed calf in the gap between the top of your sock and the bottom of your trousers and if you sit on the back of your jacket, it will not ride up over your shoulders and make you look hunchbacked.

Make-up is essential for television – without it you'll look like you've been up drinking all night. The camera makes you look pasty and off-colour, but make-up can make your face look 'normal' to the viewer. The make-up artist can also do wonders with five o-clock shadow, bags under the eyes, shiny foreheads, spots and blemishes. Tony Benn recalls Labour leader Huge Gaitskell's early outings in television in the 1950s, when the make-up artist 'took tremendous care to obliterate his double chin and remove the bags and even shorten the long upper lip.'

It is comforting to know that the next time you watch Jack Straw, Simon Hughes or Michael Portillo in full flow on *Newsnight*, they are all made up like a bunch of teenage girls on a hen night.

Types of Interview

There are different type of media interview, each requiring a slightly different approach:

Television

- Live television interview – you plus the presenter (*Newsnight*, TV news)
- Pre-recorded television – a clip of you talking, no presenter (TV News)
- Studio discussion – you, the presenter and one or two others (Late night political programmes)

- Live or pre-recorded studio discussion, with audience (*Question Time*)
- Location – on a building site, hospital, school, or anywhere (TV News)
- Doorstep – as you're running for cover (TV News, *Cook Report*)

Radio
- Live interview, in studio (*Today* programme, radio news, Jimmy Young)
- Live, down a telephone line, or 'down the line' (radio news)
- Live studio discussion (Talk Radio)
- Live or pre-recorded studio discussion, with audience (*Any Questions*)
- Recorded, down the line, into a tape recorder, or in a studio (radio news)
- Phone-in – in a studio, with members of the public phoning in (daytime radio).

Interview technique
At a location, you will interviewed then and there, so watch out for distractions and noise in the background. You might be outside, or even in the rain, but try not to look cold or wet. Be sure to remove outside gear like gloves, hats and scarves. Remember to look at the interviewer, not the camera.

If you are appearing in a studio, the style is very different. You arrive at the studio. You might have been chauffeured there by the programme. You will be taken by a researcher or production assistant into the 'green room' which is where guests and interviewers mingle before the interview. If it is an evening programme like *Newsnight*, there will be plenty of food and drink – but avoid anything alcoholic, you need to stay sharp. Enjoy the free booze afterwards if there's time. You'll be taken to make-up and given the full treatment. On *Today*, there's always toast and coffee and the morning papers. At this stage, you might meet whoever you are appearing with, and that gives you the opportunity to find out what they might say. You might even agree a line of argument to explore – 'you say this ... I'll say that'.

On a television programme you'll be taken into the studio and wired up with a microphone. The seats will seem hard and the lights bright. On a radio programme, you will be taken into the studio for the few minutes you are being interviewed and removed swiftly afterwards.

The overriding impression is one of speed. You will feel that your interview went in no time at all. That is why it is essential to express your points at the start, because there will be little time to spare. Get your soundbite out into the open immediately, so that interviewer and other guests must respond to your points not the other way round. Drag the discussion on to your territory. Seize the initiative.

Don't seek to answer the interviewer's question, but instead see the question as a cue to say what you came to say. The question is merely the invitation for you to start talking. You must stick to your agreed line, and not allow the interviewer to lead you off in directions you don't want to go in. If you attempt to answer each question, the interview will be over before you have had a chance to say what you wanted, and you will have been thwarted. If the interview is a debate between you and another person, try to monopolise as much time as possible. The longer you talk, the less time your opponent has for his or her carefully crafted soundbite. The programme producers up in the studio gallery will try to direct the cameras to broadcast whoever is speaking, so make sure it's you. If you wait patiently, the interview will be over.

Avoid wild hand gestures or violent head movements – you should try to stay static, but not wooden. At all costs, avoid raising your voice. Some interviewers will try and needle you to provoke a reaction. If they succeed, they have some great television or radio, but you have lost your credibility. If the interviewer is getting excited, use slow, calm sentences to respond and lower the temperature. Look at the way Michael Howard kept his cool, just, under the sustained barrage of Jeremy Paxman asking about the sacking of prison boss Derek Lewis. If the other guy loses his temper but you do not, you have won.

If the interview is focussing on the wrong issues – and wrong means issues where you are weak or unsure – try to bring the discussion round to your preferred subject. Try a phrase like 'what people really want to know is ... ' or 'what you should be asking is ... '

If the interviewer tries to ask the same question, stick to your guns and don't stray off-message.

Always try to get the last word, so that you leave a lasting impression. All this may sound rude and aggressive, but if it is done with a smile and aplomb, you will be hailed as having given a good interview.

Afterwards, when the make-up has been removed, and you've returned to normality, you should ask a trusted adviser what they thought, and hope for an honest reaction. If you can watch the video or hear the tape, you may learn about what you did well and what you got wrong, and so give a better interview next time.

Television debates

During the past few general elections there has been speculation about whether the party leaders would engage in a televised debate. The televised debate has been a highlight of American Presidential elections for over forty years. The 1960 television contest between John F. Kennedy and Richard Nixon is viewed as a classic of the genre. Kennedy – calm, in control, and made-up for the cameras won the debate with Nixon, who looked unshaven, sweaty and shifty. It was Kennedy's television skills which won the day, not his policies. Significantly, the radio audience, hearing the same debate without the visuals, thought that Richard Nixon was the winner.

It is hard to see how the television debate formula would work in the British electoral context. Our general elections are a series of local constituency elections, not a national contest for Prime Minister, despite the creeping presidential nature of our politics. We also have a third party nationally, in the shape of the Liberal Democrats, and strong contenders in Scotland and Wales in the Scottish National Party and Plaid Cymru, so a straight head-to-head between Tory and Labour leaders would exclude other shades of electoral opinion.

In the lead-up to the 2001 general election, speculation started to mount about the opportunity for a televised debate. The Tories pressed for one. The Prime Minister's Spokesman, Alastair Campbell, hinted that Tony Blair might agree, as a way of generating more interest in politics. For Tony Blair to agree to a debate with William Hague would have been extremely high-risk. Such a debate, by its nature, favours the challenger, not the incumbent. It places both men on an equal footing, so why should a Prime Minister place himself in such a position when he can campaign with all the advantages of office. It is impossible to imagine, for example, Margaret Thatcher acceding to a debate with Michael Foot or Neil Kinnock during the eighties. She would have had none of it.

The format of a debate is gladiatorial and combative, and favours the politician who can thrive in the atmosphere of the Oxford Union or House of Commons debate. William Hague has proved that he is good in these situations, especially at Prime Minister's Questions on a Wednesday afternoon. It is likely that Hague would be impressive in a television debate in a way that he is not in other scenarios. But even Hague has been getting advice to avoid such a show-down, for fear of Tony Blair and Charles Kennedy (who would presumably have to appear as well) ganging up on him.

No Prime Minister can be seen to be 'running scared' of a debate with the opposition. If a political leader can be labelled 'chicken' they will be followed around for the whole campaign by people in chicken suits. If such a challenge is made, it must be answered. So the most likely result was that Labour would say they wanted a debate on television with William Hague, and then create enough obstacles during the negotiations by arguing over the format, place, timing and so on, so that polling day comes around without the debate taking place. And that, funnily enough, is what happened.

Photo-opportunities

Photos are a direct and simple way of communicating a message, making a point, in telling a story. A well thought-through photo can communicate your campaign messages better than a hundred news releases. Campaign teams spend a great deal of time thinking about photo-opportunities, because of their importance in establishing a theme or creating an image of the candidate. Pictures can say more than words, in a way which is more accessible to more people, and which lasts in the popular memory.

A good example is the Queen Mother. The Queen Mother has the kind of popular support politicians can only dream of. Virtually everyone has a good impression of her. She appears regularly on television. Yet who can remember her ever saying anything? Her image is built around the impression we have of her, created purely by visual images, never spoken words. (This is one reason why the makers of *Spitting Image* gave her a brummie accent, because no-one knew what she actually sounded like.)

Churchill, as well as being the master of the soundbite and the new mass medium of radio, was a master of the photo-opportunity. He used newspaper and magazine photos and cinema newsreels to project his image. During the war, he appeared with guns, tanks, ships, soldiers, and in one famous photo, brandishing a machine-gun. In the 1945 election he used softer, home-front images such as meeting a mother and triplets.

No politician leaves to chance the ways in which they will be photographed. Labour learnt the lesson during the 1983 general election when Labour Leader Michael Foot was photographed in a variety of unfortunate ways, as John O'Farrell recalls: 'photographers from the *Sun* would follow him round hospitals and wait till he was standing next to the sign saying "Psychiatric Ward" or whatever. 'Could you move to your left please Mr Foot, we want to get you under the sign saying "Terminal Cases Only". Then he would head off to the next photo-inopportunity.'

Neil Kinnock as Labour leader in the eighties began to turn things round. Instead of being photographed with depressing backdrops – closed factories, crumbling hospitals – he used upbeat, lively, modern settings and celebrities to persuade voters Labour was the party of success and the future.

Sometimes even the most wary spin doctor has missed a trick. When Prime Minister Margaret Thatcher was photographed, alone, in an industrial wasteland in the North East of England, the photo was supposed to be an illustration of the Tories' desire for urban regeneration – but it looked like Thatcher was simply surveying the damage she had caused, like a General after a battle. The photo ended up as the cover of Gordon Brown's book *Where there is Greed*. When Tony Blair and Mo Mowlam addressed a Labour Party members' meeting in Hammersmith Town Hall in summer 2000, the shadows fell against the backdrop in such a way that a photographer managed to get a shot of what appeared to be Tony Blair's shadow throttling Mo Mowlam. It was naturally this picture which most photo-editors chose to publish the next day.

So what makes a good photo-opportunity? The message should be simple. Do not attempt complicated visual metaphors and coded signals; you are not designing a Beatles album cover. Go for simple images which convey one of your campaign themes or messages. Party leaders like to metaphorically wrap themselves in the Union Jack. Tony Blair made an appearance at the white cliffs of Dover at the last election. Margaret Thatcher used photo-ops with tanks, or in front of aircraft hanger doors with huge Union Jacks during the eighties.

For the local papers, your photo-op must be local. Try to select recognisable local landmarks like war memorials or municipal buildings and recognisable local streets for your photos. If your story is about a new school building, or a railway station roof in need of repair, or cracks in the pavement, let the pictures tell the story.

Think about props. A giant cheque addressed to pensioners and representing Gordon Brown's increased winter fuel allowance for pensioners was sent to Labour candidates in winter 2000. During the 1997 general election, Conservative candidates wrapped themselves in red ribbon to show how business was plagued by 'red tape'. Cedric the Pig became famous in the nineties as the symbol of 'fat cat businessmen' with their snouts in the trough as part of a campaign by the union GMB.

The advice from panto is useful – look behind you. Ensure there are no signs saying exit, or words which can cut or 'cropped' by photo editors to make other, damaging words. A candidate photographed with the backdrop saying 'Vote Liberal Democrat' can be made to appear with just the word 'rat' behind them by malicious cropping.

If you are organising a photo-opportunity, make sure that you have your own camera with you in case the press photographers don't show up. If you take the photo yourself you can ensure your local media have the photograph. With the decreasing cost of digital cameras and the availability of email, photos can now be emailed electronically to newspaper picture editors minutes after the photo was taken.

Letters to the editor

Newspapers welcome 'letters to the editor' which appear on the letters page. Letters can be a good way of getting a candidate's name and message into the newspaper. Local papers usually take letters from candidates on local issues. National newspapers are harder to get into, but not impossible. The competition to appear in a serious letters page like that of the *Times* is fierce, because of the stature and authority of the publication, and the large number of people who want to be read on that page.

A letter usually picks up on an issue covered in the pages of the newspaper, and makes reference to the article and the date of publication. You should also clearly mark your letter 'for publication' so the editor knows you want to see the letter in print. If you are writing to complain or clarify a mistake, but do not want to be published, put 'not for publication' at the top. You should also include contact details so that you can be phoned. The *Times* letter page will always phone its contributors to confirm that the letter has only been sent to the *Times*, and to agree edits to the text.

What letters editors are looking for is a snappy, fresh, thought-provoking view on the issue rather than the 'party line'. You can try humour or even a one-liner as a way of getting published. The shorter your letter is, the better chance it has.

Sometimes a letter to the editor can be an appeal, such as the candidate appealing on behalf of a local charity or campaign or the British Legion poppy appeal; sometimes the letter can have joint-signatories or even a list of several well-known supporters to add weight to the campaign or argument. This kind of heavyweight letter can often attract coverage in the news pages of the same newspaper, especially if the issue is controversial such as legalisation of cannabis or the single European currency.

Once your letter has appeared, you should encourage your supporters to write in, agreeing with you, or even disagreeing with you, in order to keep your name and your issue in subsequent editions. If a letters editor receives more than a handful of letters on a subject, they assume there is a groundswell of opinion and are happy to give it space.

Features and 'your shout' articles

You can try to place feature articles about issues of concern in the newspapers. National papers have the space for feature articles about politics, but also have plenty of people to write them, although many politicians such as Roy Hattersley, have second careers as journalists. Local papers tend not to take heavyweight political 'think pieces'. You need a strong local angle.

Many papers have a 'soapbox' or 'your shout' feature, whereby campaigners and those with an axe to grind are given place to have their say on an issue. This might be a good way to keep your name in the paper.

Diary columns

Most politicians dread appearing in the newspapers' diary columns. They are seldom filled with stories praising politicians' great public works or awesome intelligence. These columns appear in most newspapers, and are the place where scurrilous conjecture, unfounded rumour and unnecessary tittle-tattle about the great and the good finds a home away from the serious, responsible journalism of the news and comment pages.

Some foolhardy souls feed diary columns information (like the police, they pay for information they can use) and some even encourage their own appearance as a way of getting noticed. The politicians who want to appear in diaries tend to be fairly unimportant, but Ministers will return the call of a diary columnist, at least if they know what's good for them. Diary columnists are amoral, and owe a debt of loyalty to no-one, so if you are known to a diary column you are just as likely to be on the wrong end of a diary story as your opponent.

Sam Leith, editor of the *Peterborough* column in the *Telegraph* says that diarists are 'petty, vindictive and babyish. If you ignore their phone calls or treat them in a high-handed way, they'll find something disparaging to say about you.'

You should always treat them with respect, because despite the frivolous nature of their inquiry or the low regard you may have for this form of journalism, they have the power and opportunity to run on-going vendettas, create nicknames which stick, and trash your reputation. Those working for certain Ministers have been victims of this kind of incessant, unfair and unfunny treatment.

The best advice for those contemplating entering the world of the diary is to take a long spoon.

Rapid rebuttal

Rapid rebuttal is the technique of having your answer to your opponent's public comments or remarks in front of journalists fast enough for the journalist to cover the story in a balanced way. If your opponent says you will put taxes up, the journalists covering the election have your 'rebuttal' – your reply to the charge – in their hands, showing that you are pledged not to raise income taxes, but that your opponent's plans would mean higher taxes for people.

Rapid rebuttal is a product of the speed with which the media now moves. Political campaign teams must act fast because news bulletins are put together in minutes and news programmes are now 'rolling' – or constantly on the air. The days are long gone when a political campaign team could spend the afternoon checking the facts, thinking about a suitable answer to their critics, tracking down and clearing the response with a politician, and then sending it over to a journalist. Political events, especially during a campaign, are often covered live. The reaction to a major speech or news conference is instant. There is no space for deliberation or consultation. Politicians and their advisers must think on their feet, and put forceful arguments, without the danger of gaffes, with only seconds to think.

Rapid rebuttal is reliant on the fast and accurate information retrieval systems, which modern information technology can today deliver. Databases of information can be stored and cross-referenced with every speech, manifesto, election address, pamphlet, book, newspaper article, and transcript of interviews that a public figure has been responsible for going back over decades. Words uttered in an Oxford Union debate or in the pages of *Tribune* twenty years ago can come back to haunt senior politicians. The Labour Party's system is called Excalibur (the sword of truth).

The technique was honed into an art form in the US Democrats campaign in 1992, whereby Bill Clinton's response to a George Bush speech was in front of the journalists before Bush had even resumed his seat. The story became, not Bush's speech, but Bush's reaction to Clinton's rebuttal of the speech, all within 20 minutes of the speech being delivered. The spin doctors George Stephanopolous and James Carville would sit at the centre of the war room in Little Rock watching a major Bush speech, being fed facts and figures by a team of researchers, deciding 'the line', and phoning their contacts in the media, all within minutes.

British political parties have studied and learnt from the American experience. Strategists from both Labour and Tories were present during the Presidential campaigns in 1992, 1996, and 2000. The Tories side with the Republicans, and the Labour people with the Democrats. In 2000, Labour staffers volunteered to help Hillary Clinton's election bid in New York state. British political campaigns reflect the contours of the British electoral system, but the influence of US campaigning techniques, where their application is relevant, is being increasingly felt in Britain.

The tricks journalists play

When researching my first book, *Be Your Own Spin Doctor*, I phoned a journalist friend to ask about the tricks journalists play to get information out of people who don't want to give it. 'There are no tricks' he said 'just good journalism'. However, whether it is defined as good journalism or simply trickery, there are techniques journalists will use on candidates and their campaign teams in order to get them to say things they should not say.

The first is to ascribe quotes to candidates in words which have never passed their lips. The technique is simple. If a journalist makes a statement to you and you agree with it, or even fail to robustly disagree, the statement can be written up and published as your statement. If a journalist prefaces a statement with 'would you say that ... ' you must be aware that all that follows can be printed under your name as though you had said it.

For example if a journalist says 'would you say that your party leader has a face like a baboon and his policies stink like one' and you fail to reject the allegation or simply laugh, the next days newspaper might contain a story like this:

Leader is 'baboon', claims candidate

Political candidate Fred Smith shocked the local political scene last night with an astonishing attack on his own party leader. Smith, 33, claimed his leader 'had a face like a baboon' and that the party's policies 'stank.'

His political rival Joan Smith said 'this shows that the other party is split top to bottom. This descent into petty name-calling proves you can't trust them.'

Mr Smith was unavailable for comment.

The only way to deal with the 'would you say ... ' trick is to be absolutely clear with the journalist that the words he has used are not your words, and that those views cannot be ascribed to you. Be very clear. And then give the journalist a quote which they can use, which accurately reflects your campaign message.

Journalists can use the Pinter Pause – whereby they introduce long pauses into their conversations with you. The idea is that you will want to fill the embarrassing gaps in conversation by blurting out whatever comes into your head, giving away more than you intended. The answer to the Pinter Pause is to stay silent – whoever speaks first loses.

Sometimes they will pretend they know more about an issue than they do, or make you think they have been chatting with your Agent or party campaign managers, to lull you into a false sense of security so that you give away information. A journalist might reveal something personal about themselves ('Nothing I like better after a hard day at work than to go home and drink a bottle of gin by myself – I expect you like a drink too?') in the hope that you will reveal some vice or another.

One technique of interviewing is the Columbo killer question – where a 'soft' interview is ended with a 'killer question' when you are off your guard, using the technique of the bumbling television detective.

Complaining

If you are unhappy with the coverage you receive because it is biased, not fair or accurate, or because you have been misrepresented, you should complain. Complaining about poor journalism is one way to get better coverage next time. If an inaccuracy is allowed to stand, it may become established and hard to deny later on down the road. In the first instance, you should complain to the journalist responsible for the offending article or story, and their news editor. You can demand a retraction and apology. If they are obviously in the wrong, they have a duty to print an apology. If the local route does not satisfy your complaint, you can take it to the Press Complaints Commission which adjudicates in disputes with the media.

Spinning out of control?

Spin is a modern media obsession, but there is little evidence that the voters share that fascination. Media management, or even manipulation, is vital to the modern campaign, because through the media we contact the voters. But for political parties what really matters is trust, credibility, and for those in office, delivering on their promises. Spin is no substitute for substance, and as every advertiser knows, all the packaging in the world cannot disguise a duff product.

Top tips for dealing with the media

1 Treat journalists with respect, give them stories, respect their deadlines, and thank them when they get it right
2 Always return their calls, even if you don't want to
3 Be a purveyor of news not a nuisance-caller
4 Keep your contacts hot and up-to-date
5 Think about photos, letters, articles not just news releases
6 Take swift action if you are misrepresented – use rapid rebuttal
7 Use exclusives – but spread the favours round
8 Do interviews – but prepare thoroughly and never look directly into the camera
9 Be nice to juniors – soon they'll be seniors
10 Keep your press cuttings and let everyone see them
11 Through the media you can reach millions.

6 Indirect Campaigning II: Other Forms of Communication

Advertising and posters

Political campaigners have been fixing posters and notices to walls for public consumption since the beginning of democratic politics. In recent years, it is the Tories who have produced some of the most effective political posters, notably as a result of their hiring of Saatchi and Saatchi in the late seventies.

In the 1979 election, their 'Labour Isn't Working' poster showing an unemployment queue was particularly effective, not to say ironic, as unemployment soared to three million after the Tories' victory. Throughout the eighties, the Tories' posters were bold and powerful. 'Labour's Policy on Arms' showed a soldier with his arms held up in surrender. Labour's 'Double Whammy' of higher prices and higher taxes was a boxer with huge gloves. The 'Labour Tax Bombshell' showed a huge bomb. I remember first setting eyes on the Tax Bombshell poster during the 1992 campaign, on a strategically-placed hoarding at the top of Walworth Road where Labour had its headquarters. My heart sank when I realised how effective it would be.

Only in the early and mid-eighties, with the success of the Greater London Council's advertising campaign against its own abolition, did the left learn to love advertising. Labour's posters grew in sophistication during the nineties. In 1992 Norman Lamont was portrayed as VAT man. In 1997, Labour's election pledges were each displayed on a series of brightly coloured posters. The Tories were attacked for '22 tax rises' and the slogan 'Enough is Enough'.

Posters can be used as part of a national advertising campaign, with adverts on poster sites targeted on key seats, and in national and local newspapers and magazines. This is very costly. They can also be used for photo-opportunities, with a politician unveiling the new poster to the media, in the hope that photographs of the poster will appear in the newspapers and on television. Sometimes, where money is tight, a single poster can be produced in the hope of winning media coverage.

Posters can be used as part of your door-to-door campaign activity. Candidates usually have an election poster with their name, party name and logo and party colours which supporters can put up in the window. In households containing different allegiances, two or more posters may appear in the windows of the same house. In recent by-elections 'swing' voters have been encouraged with posters which say 'Lib Dem Voting Labour' or vice versa. This technique was pioneered during the Monmouth by-election in 1990 by Labour wanting to attract votes from the Liberal Democrats.

Posters can be distributed early to supporters, and appear across the constituency as soon as the election is called, creating an immediate impact . A poster which is sent out with double-sided sellotape already affixed stands a much better chance of being used than one where the person has to look for blu-tack. In parliamentary constituencies, you can decide which parts of the constituency have the highest traffic flow and the main roads, and cross-reference those areas with the addresses of your supporters. Those people can be asked to display posters so that the maximum number of people see them. In urban seats, you can work out which roads lead to marginal and key seats, so that posters in one constituency can help the campaign profile in another. As well as posters, you can use 'flying V' boards, like estate agent boards on shops for rent, or garden flags, which are like estate agent 'for sale' signs. There will be DIY enthusiasts or carpenters in your local campaign team who can be sent out to put the big poster sites up as soon as the starting gun is fired.

Philip Gould is disparaging about the effect of political advertising: 'Advertising has an effect, but it is small and rarely decisive.' He points to the evidence that the Tories spent twice as much as Labour in 1997 on advertising, but comprehensively lost the election.

But the effect cannot be wholly negated. As part of a co-ordinated campaign, with messages being repeated across a range of media, posters and advertising can help build a campaign and influence perceptions, and ultimately, voting behaviour.

Posters come in all shapes and sizes ...

Top tips for posters

1 Put posters where the greatest number of people will see them
2 Refresh the posters during the campaign
3 Remove defaced or damaged posters
4 Go for bold colours and big text
5 Unveil your poster for the media
6 Try for Flying Vs and garden flags
7 Take down your posters after the campaign.

Newsletters and leaflets

Local newsletters and leaflets have a role to play in the modern campaign, but should not form the sole form of communications with the electorate because their effectiveness is doubtful compared to other forms of communication, especially personal contact. Leaflets and newsletters can have the advantage, with the spread of desk-top publishing systems like Adobe PageMaker and Microsoft Publisher and cheap colour printing and photocopying, of being highly localised, direct, and contemporary. They can be produced by campaign teams in a matter of hours to respond to events as they happen, and can be produced for distribution to a few hundred target voters.

The Liberal Democrats' *Focus* newsletter stands as the example of localised newsletters for others to follow. *Focus* is produced by local Liberal Democrat parties and regularly distributed to their target areas, in particular seats, wards or even streets. Mark Glover, a former Lib Dem campaigner, now with the Labour Party, identifies the following characteristics of the *Focus* newsletter: '*Focus* uses local place names in its title to give people a sense of ownership, but uses the main name *Focus* all over the country, so if someone moves to a different area, the local *Focus* seems familiar. It always has tick-boxes and "grumble sheets" for return to the local "*Focus* team", to create the impression of listening, but which actually serve as a way of identifying local concerns and capturing names and addresses of potential local voters. Where possible, the size and shape of the newsletter looks like the local paper. The issues are always highly localised – potholes and cracked pavements. *Focus* assumes a high level of intelligence, but a low level of knowledge.'

To increase the effectiveness of newsletters, frequency is the key. It is better to post a newsletter through 250 doors four times a year than through 1000 doors once a year, because the regularity will generate familiarity, and therefore acceptance. If photographs can be included, these should contain familiar local locations and landmarks, and real local people that others will know. Stories should be short and snappy with eye-catching headlines – your newsletters should be more tabloid than *Telegraph*.

Leaflets and newsletters should contain a message, either in the photograph or in the headline, which can be absorbed and understood, even subliminally, in the ten seconds it takes to pick up the newsletter from the doormat and walk to the bin, or the few seconds from being handed one in the street to shoving it into a pocket.

Leaflets can be localised and targeted. A leaflet can be produced for a leaflet drop at a particular time and a particular place, for example a railway station in the morning rush hour. Leaflets can be targeted at the morning commuters, with messages directly relevant to them and their circumstances. The leaflets can say 'Good morning'; they can refer to the state of the railways, and the name of the station. Here, a leaflet which is one-colour and photocopied, but which is targeted accurately, can be more effective than a glossy leaflet designed for general distribution. In local elections, glossy leaflets can smack of over-professionalisation and the interference of national party machines. Often they become mingled with leaflets for pizza delivery on the doormat and stand more chance of being ignored or thrown away than a leaflet of less quality. Something which looks well-designed and attractive, but is obviously locally-produced, with a local place name clearly at the top is more likely to be read.

Leaflets need to be simple, direct, obvious and easy to comprehend in a few seconds. They should contain some kind of response mechanism – a tear-off and return slip, an email address or a hotline number – so that people can respond if they feel a desire to do so, but do not expect more than a tiny percentage of your leaflets to elicit a response.

The design should aid, not hinder the communication. Avoid heavy blocks of text and confusing 'arty' layouts. Use simple typefaces (or 'fonts') throughout – choose one for headlines such as Arial or Franklin Gothic, and another such as Times or Times Roman for the text. Do not

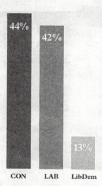

Rose

Chester

News from
Christine Russell
Labour Party
Campaign Hotline
0990 133311
Per minute 1.0p peak 5p Off peak 2.5p/anytime

HOW WE'VE BEEN BETRAYED BY THE TORIES

The people of Chester have been betrayed by the Tories. Many people who voted Tory at the last General Election are now saying, 'Never again!'

They PROMISED to cut taxes but instead introduced 22 separate tax increases, costing a typical Chester family £2,120 a year.

The Tories PROMISED to cut crime but it has doubled since 1980 and many people in Chester live in fear of crime.

The Tories PROMISED to cut red tape in the NHS but their internal market has cost the

CHRISTINE RUSSELL LABOUR'S LOCAL CANDIDATE

Countess of Chester hospital over £1 million – enough for 60 extra nurses.

No wonder people are saying, 'Never again!'

New Labour has the energy, commitment and leadership to meet the challenge of improving the quality of life for ALL and not the few.

new **Labour** new **Britain**

Only Labour Can Beat The Conservatives

Labour only needs a small swing to overturn the Tory majority in Chester. The Lib Dems have very little support here – as shown by the result last time.

CON	LAB	LibDem
44%	42%	13%

Different styles of leaflets

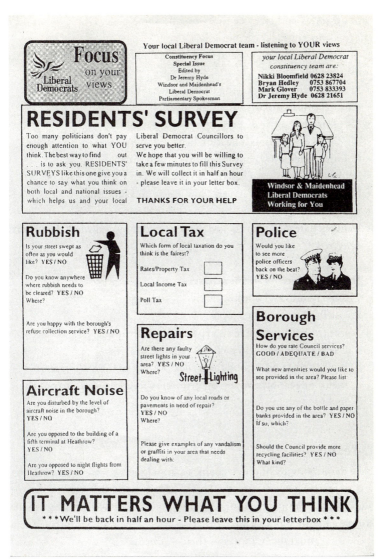

Focus on your views
Liberal Democrats

Your local Liberal Democrat team - listening to YOUR views

Constituency Focus
Special Issue
Edited by
Dr Jeremy Hyde
Windsor and Maidenhead's
Liberal Democrat
Parliamentary Spokesman

your local Liberal Democrat
constituency team are:

Nikki Bloomfield 0628 23824
Bryan Hedley 0753 867704
Mark Glover 0753 833393
Dr Jeremy Hyde 0628 21651

RESIDENTS' SURVEY

Too many politicians don't pay enough attention to what YOU think. The best way to find out . . . is to ask you. RESIDENTS' SURVEYS like this one give you a chance to say what you think on both local and national issues - which helps us and your local

Liberal Democrat Councillors to serve you better.
We hope that you will be willing to take a few minutes to fill this Survey in. We will collect it in half an hour - please leave it in your letter box.

THANKS FOR YOUR HELP

Windsor & Maidenhead
Liberal Democrats
Working for You

Rubbish

Is your street swept as often as you would like? YES / NO

Do you know anywhere where rubbish needs to be cleared? YES / NO
Where?

Are you happy with the borough's refuse collection service? YES / NO

Local Tax

Which form of local taxation do you think is the fairest?

Rates/Property Tax [ ]

Local Income Tax [ ]

Poll Tax [ ]

Repairs

Are there any faulty street lights in your area? YES / NO
Where?
Street Lighting

Do you know of any local roads or pavements in need of repair?
YES / NO
Where?

Please give examples of any vandalism or graffiti in your area that needs dealing with:

Police

Would you like to see more police officers back on the beat? YES / NO

Borough Services

How do you rate Council services?
GOOD / ADEQUATE / BAD

What new amenities would you like to see provided in the area? Please list

Do you use any of the bottle and paper banks provided in the area? YES / NO
If so, which?

Should the Council provide more recycling facilities? YES / NO
What kind?

Aircraft Noise

Are you disturbed by the level of aircraft noise in the borough?
YES / NO

Are you opposed to the building of a fifth terminal at Heathrow?
YES / NO

Are you opposed to night flights from Heathrow? YES / NO

IT MATTERS WHAT YOU THINK

* * * We'll be back in half an hour - Please leave this in your letterbox * * *

mix up styles and sizes of fonts on the same page. Don't be afraid of space – sometimes less is more.

If you are ordering printed material such as leaflets or brochures you must specify:

- Artwork – are you supplying it, and in what format?
- Photographs – are they camera-ready?
- Text – in what software package?
- Binding – does your publication need a staple or glue?
- Colours – including pantone numbers and tints
- Folds – how many and where?
- Paper – what 'stock' of paper? How glossy and how thick?
- How many?
- Delivery date and address – when you need it by and where you want it delivered.

Top tips for leaflets and newsletters
1   Keep it local and not too glossy
2   Use local places and people
3   Use the KISS principle – Keep It Short and Simple
4   Use big headlines and pictures
5   If it can't be understood from the doormat to the bin, forget it
6   Include a tear-off coupon or 'grumble sheet' for people to return
7   Include a phone number and email addresss

Direct mail

New databasing technology enables campaigners to use direct mail as a way of reaching voters directly. This is usually hand-delivered to a named address by a campaign volunteer. In one way, a campaign direct mail is simply a highly sophisticated form of leaflet – one which is targeted to an individual and directly addresses their concerns.

To be successful, direct mail must appear as personal as possible, because all of us have an aversion to the 'junk mail' which clogs up our hallways. It is easy to use databases to create 'mail merge' letters which contain a person's name and address; to work, these must be 100 per cent accurate. A misspelled name or wrongly assigned sex is worse than no name.

Labour campaigning leaflet

Letters can be directed to particular geographical areas, or interest groups. People who have signed petitions against animal cruelty can be targeted with direct mail letters addressing their concerns. Members of a faith group or ethnic minority can be written to by a respected community leader in support of the candidate. Ethnic minority languages can be used. First-time voters can be targeted. If the voter is a switcher, letters can be sent from those who have switched offering the reassurances they need to tip them over the edge. Letters can be made to appear as if they are from famous political leaders, complete with what appear to be hand-written signatures.

The content should be simple and direct. There should be a clear proposition – why the voter should support the candidate, why the other side would be a disaster, and what the recipient can do to ensure victory. Other details should be included, such as how to get a postal or proxy vote, where the local polling station is, what days and what times the polling station is open, and how to contact the local campaign office. There should be some e-friendly information such as an email address and a website address.

I saw a marketing device where an article from a magazine had been torn out and sent to named recipients with a post-it note attached with a hand-written note saying 'thought you'd be interested in this' with an illegible scribble of a name. Most people would read the note and assume it was someone they knew, and bother to look at the article. In fact, the article, post-it note and signature were all fakes, but it made people read the messages in a way an anonymous piece of junk mail would not. Marketeers are using direct mail in preference to media advertising because of the capability it has for accurate targeting. Some companies, such as Heinz, have moved their marketing 'spend' away from mass marketing to targeted marketing. As the techniques become ever-more sophisticated, and as political campaigning becomes ever-more personalised, politics will emulate this trend.

Campaign songs

Campaigns will often adopt a song or piece of music as their theme for the election. John F. Kennedy in 1960 had 'High Hopes' from the musical *High*

Society. John Major and Neil Kinnock chose stirring classical music to provide the background to their campaigns. Bill Clinton opted for the baby-boomer favourite 'Don't Stop Thinking About Tomorrow' by Fleetwood Mac. Al Gore went for 'You Ain't Seen Nothing Yet'. Tony Blair's campaign song in 1997 was 'Things can only get better.'

At the 2000 Labour Party conference, the theme song was Roxy Music's 'Let's Work Together', which was tipped to be their campaign song for the 2001 general election.

The choice of music must reflect the kind of campaign messages you want to project and the voters you most want to appeal to. Classical music may imply stature and statesmanship, but pop music can confer modernity and momentum. One piece of advice for those choosing a campaign theme song – pick a piece of music that you can listen to a million times, because like the Queen and the National Anthem, you will, and pick something that you don't mind hating by the end of the campaign.

Party election broadcasts

When the TV announcers used to say 'there now follows a party political broadcast on behalf of the Conservative/Labour/Liberal Party, which will also be shown on all other channels' it was code for 'this may be boring, but there's no point changing channel.' Party Political Broadcasts, now restricted to election campaigns, party conferences and the Budget, were cult viewing. They were the few minutes a year when political parties were allowed to put their case free from interference, usually with hilarious results.

The earliest PPBs were Cholmley-Warner style politicians behind desks talking direct to the viewer. Tony Benn starred in Labour's 1959 general election broadcasts as the *faux*-presenter of 'Britain Belongs to You' alongside Woodrow Wyatt and Christopher Mayhew. These PEBs were designed to look like real current affairs programmes, and for the time, were impressive. As Tony Benn recalled 'I fought a brilliant campaign, and lost.'

Often the content was desperately patronising. Shirley Williams would show us her shopping basket to make a point about price increases under the Tories. Margaret Thatcher, in her late-seventies Margot Leadbetter days, would lecture us on 'I know how you must feel.' In 1987, Labour managed to produce a work of genius. What became known as 'Kinnock, the Movie' was a brilliant example of how political broadcasting should work – passionate, inspirational, with high production values, and not a shopping basket in sight. The same year, however, Labour also produced possibly their worst PPB, with Glenda Jackson in a potting shed using pot plants to make a point about British manufacturing and foreign imports. For example, Japanese imports were represented by a Bonsai tree. Good grief.

The Americans have always done it better. Because the only restriction on political broadcasting is the size of your wallet, the Republicans and Democrats slug it out with political 'spots' or adverts, which respond to one another week by week. In the fifties, US political advertising reflected the terrible nature of mainstream advertising. Fifties voters were asked for their support with catchy tunes and rhymes. Adlai Stevenson's 1952 presidential challenge was backed by a song which contained the lyrics 'Adlai – we love you madly' and 'He's the Gov we love'. Eisenhower fared little better. In 1956, his campaign song was 'Hang out the banner and beat the drum, we'll take Ike to Wash-ing-ton.' In 1964, things had turned a little more serious. The famous Lyndon Johnson spot showed a little girl counting the petals on a flower, followed by a countdown to a nuclear explosion. Ronald Reagan used the Cold War theme in 1984 with his 'There's a Bear in the Woods' spot.

Themes in American political adverts often later appear in British ones. George McGovern was shown in 1972 as having 'two faces' to highlight his inconsistent views, and the Tories did the same to Neil Kinnock by showing his head spinning round. Reagan's slogan for re-election in 1984 'Now our country is turning around – why would we want to turn back?' is sure to be echoed in Labour's bid for re-election in 2001. Clinton campaigned in 1992 on the slogan 'enough is enough' as did Blair in 1997.

American TV adverts can also be vicious about their opponents in a way the British have still to catch up with. In 1988, Dukakis was pulverised by the Bush campaign's use of a single episode when Dukakis was Governor. A convicted murderer, Willie Horton, was released from prison under the state furlough scheme, and went on to murder and rape while away from prison. Bush blamed Dukakis's 'revolving door' prison policy, and ran TV adverts which showed prisoners leaving prison through a revolving door.

To qualify for an election broadcast, your party must field candidates in at least 50 constituencies. This rule allows fringe parties such as the Natural Law Party, the Liberal Party (not the Lib Dems) and the Green Party access to television. In 1997, eight parties without any Members of Parliament were allowed broadcasts. The British National Party cheated in 1997 in their attempts to gain a television broadcast by forging the nomination papers for candidates to qualify under the 50-seat rule.

(For a fine selection of broadcasts, see the videos *Party Political Broadcasts Greatest Hits, 1953–97* and *American Campaign Commercials 1952–96*, both published by Politico's Publishing.)

Manifestos

Manifestos are the guides to action that a political party and candidate promise to enact if elected. Manifestos are the contract with the voters, against which the performance of governments can be judges. They are drawn up by parties to attract support and answer questions by detailing the policies and issues which are the most salient and which define contemporary politics. Manifestos have ceased to be the most important element of the campaign, and they are read only by a tiny percentage of the electorate, despite being on sale in newsagents and bookshops. They still matter because they set the tone of an election campaign and help define the battleground, particularly via discussion in the media. Parties go to some trouble to launch their manifesto with a bang, and the launch is part of the ritual of a general election. Often manifestos are short on detailed policy pronouncements, and merely set out broad objectives. The Conservatives' 1979 manifesto hardly featured privatisation, which became the defining characteristic of Thatcher's Governments.

The most famous manifesto of recent times is Labour's 1983 general election manifesto, which was famously described by Gerald Kaufman as 'the longest suicide note in history.' The manifesto was the result of a sustained period of internal warfare in the Labour Party, and showed that the left-wing of the party was in ascendancy. At the 'Clause II meeting' which finalises Labour's manifestos, Labour right-wingers such as John Golding made no attempt to moderate the red-blooded nature of the policies in order to give the left-wingers enough rope to hang themselves. The resulting document, 'The New Hope for Britain', with its promises to raise taxes, withdraw from the EEC, scrap nuclear weapons, and nationalise key industries frightened the life out of the electorate, but was welcomed by the Conservatives, who bought copies in bulk to distribute to waivering voters to ensure they didn't vote Labour. Labour's HQ even gave the Tories a discount.

The Internet

The Internet has the potential to transform political campaigning as significantly as television did in the 1950s. It may even have the capacity to transform our whole style of democracy, because it gives people the ability to communicate with other people, directly, personally, and without the need for hierarchy, mediation or censorship. In this sense, for the first time mass communications has the potential to be democratic, not controlled by one class, one coterie of media barons, or subject to controls by states or individuals.

Devised by the US military, the Internet has worked in ways which its inventors would not have expected. It has moved from a system used by academics and nerds into the communications channel which is transforming the way we work, shop, and relax.

It can provide near-instant communications with millions of people across continents. Costs for access are low, and unlike other forms of communication, the costs for producing material pose little barrier to participation. It is cheap to use and almost impossible to censor. In the UK, a third of the population already have access to the Internet and 63 per cent of the population will be online by 2003.

Just as the Internet is transforming our leisure, retail and working patterns, so the new technologies will transform our forms of protest and politics. We have already seen the power of the Internet to mobilise activists, independent from traditional political parties or structures, and unchecked by the authorities, at the 'Battle in Seattle', the anti-capitalism demonstrations in London in 1999 and the Fuel protests in September 2000.

The Internet allows you to create a campaign identity on the world wide web which can accessed by anyone with a PC and modem anywhere in the world. Your campaign messages and arguments, and notice about your events and publications can be made available to millions. You can use the Internet to create lists of supporters, to organise petitions and fundraising, and to sell and distribute campaign materials online. You can create a forum for discussion and debate, and answer questions from interested parties. Candidates can create virtual hustings and the virtual 'town hall meetings' pioneered by Bill Clinton.

Websites

Everybody has a website these days from Tescos to the Queen. Political websites are growing in size and complexity. The Number Ten Downing Street website has changed in a few months from being a tourist site with a virtual tour of the Downing Street building, to being a cornucopia of information, news releases, speeches, links to other parts of government, a kids section, and the transcripts of the regular official briefing by the Prime Minister's official spokesman to the media.

There are political sites such as YouGov.com and Politicsdirect.com which contain a wealth of material.

A website is an expression of your campaign's core messages, themes, and personality. It should be a virtual expression of all the messages you want the world to know about your campaign. MPs and candidates use their websites as another way of gaining attention and winning new support.

Millions of people may stop and have a look – it is worth getting it right. The sites which are successful are *fit-for-purpose* – in other words, ones which fulfil their purpose without trying to be too clever or over-designed.

If a site is a focal point and exchange for campaign information, then the information should be easily understood and accessible, as well as being up-to-date and tailored for use by activists. A website is an incredibly efficient way to get information to a large number of people instantly and at low cost.

Despite the temptations for a range of clever design features, do not allow clutter and over-complexity to obscure the core messages. If your site is aimed at potential supporters, the content will be more attractive and perhaps more balanced and discursive. The web is interactive and allows lateral as well as horizontal contact between supporters of your campaign – so ensure your site has discussion boards and bulletin boards to let the campaign subject come under discussion and scrutiny. You should monitor the online discussion and watch out for infiltration and hacking. When the Labour Party website was hacked into, the hackers left a link which, if you asked for details of the Cabinet, sent you straight to Jim Henson's Muppets.

Email

Email is a form of communication which places messages directly in front of an individual, unlike posters, newsletters, or media appearances. The message appears in a voter's home or office just inches from their nose. During the 2000 US Presidential elections, millions of voters were sent email messages every day by the parties. The targets were people who had expressed a desire to be kept in touch with the campaign, so they were receptive to the messages. These emails covered the political ebb and flow of the campaign, rebuttal and counter-rebuttal, commentary on the TV debates and on-going issues. As polling day neared, the emails were focussed on organisation and getting out the vote. On the day itself, a voter would receive six or seven emails during the day trying to entice them out to vote – the virtual knock-up.

As an experiment, I registered for the US Democrat email list for the 2000 elections, and throughout the campaign received information which was relevant, interesting, and not covered in the media.

For example, this one in December 2000 (see opposite).

On polling day, I was bombarded with messages telling me to vote (not much good as I didn't have a vote and I was in London). In an election where the outcome was decided by a handful of votes, whatever marginal difference to turnout these emails may have had made the difference between victory and defeat.

Interactivity unbound

But the potential of the new media is much more than simple one-way communications. What is revolutionary about the Internet is that it is interactive. Already, video clips of politicians giving their soundbites are available from the news websites. In the near-future, campaign teams will be able to offer a library of video clips of their candidates addressing

Welcome to Democratic News! December 6, 2000

****

IN THIS ISSUE
- Count Our Votes
- Support the DNC
- On the Web
- Polls and Discussions

****

COUNT OUR VOTES
CountOurVotes.com
The Florida State Legislature wants to throw out the votes of all Americans
and choose Florida's electors themselves. Find out what you can do to make
sure every vote counts at:
http://www.countourvotes.com/

****

SUPPORT THE DNC
As you can imagine, the resources of the Democratic National Committee have
been stretched to the limit. We need to quickly replenish our Party's
financial resources. Please make an urgently needed secure online
contribution to the DNC today.
http://www.democrats.org/support/

****

ON THE WEB
DEMSTUFF.COM
Now available from DemStuff.com: "Friends Don't Let Friends Vote Republican"
t-shirts. A true collectable from the 2000 election cycle. Get yours today,
and receive a free "Another Proud Democrat" bumper sticker and button. And
check out the other great deals on Democratic merchandise at DemStuff.com!
Show your Democratic pride this holiday season and purchase officially
licensed DNC political merchandise from Demstuff.com:
http://www.demstuff.com/general/specials.htm

****

the key issues of the day. When someone writes a letter to a politician on an issue, say animal experimentation, or euthanasia, the politician's staff usually send a pre-prepared letter, with the relevant name and address of the sender, addressing the issue. This enables a small number of staff to deal with a large number of letters. The Internet will allow pre-prepared video answers to questions by politicians.

It won't be long before a voter can ask a question directly to the candidates via a website with voice recognition, and a video answer will appear on their screen with the candidate answering the question. 'What's your policy on the Middle East?' the voter will ask, and the computer will instantly run the video clip with the politician's views. The technology will allow a personal 'virtual conversation' between candidate and voter. It isn't too difficult to see a situation where the video clip candidate uses the voter's own name during their conversation.

As Dick Morris says 'when a candidate can come into one's own home for a personal chat over the computer, the effect will be electrifying, just as it was when we first heard a president's voice over radio in FDR's fireside chats.'

Top tips for cyber-campaigning

1 If you're not campaigning in cyberspace, you're not campaigning at all
2 Websites should be easy to navigate and understand, not winners of design awards
3 Emails must be targeted and relevant – not 'spam'
4 Use email to circulate campaign briefings
5 Chatrooms can be targeted by your supporters
6 Use the Internet to rally your support and get out the vote
7 Keep up to date with the latest developments and let the technology help your campaign.

7   When the Wheels Come Off

'Character is destiny.'

Heraclitus

Things go wrong in politics. All the planning in the world cannot adequately prepare you for the rough and tumble of electioneering. Your opponents will endeavour to spring surprises, and the voters will always have a few surprises of their own.

Events may take over, and knock your campaign schedules for six. You may become embroiled in a scandal, or make a terrible gaffe. Sometimes the candidate can recover, sometimes not. In many cases, it is what you do to deal with a scandal or gaffe which determines whether you end up elected or end up as toast. A clever politician will use adversity to his advantage, come out fighting, and end up in a better position. What looks like an irreversible setback can be a springboard to success.

Scandals

There may be no magic formula for how to win an election, but there are plenty of ways to lose one. Politics is littered with the corpses of those exposed as fraudsters, adulterers or liars, and sometimes all three. For a politician's career to be dogged by scandal is damaging enough. For a scandal to break over the head of a candidate during an election campaign, when voters can actually show what they think of you, is disastrous.

All political careers end in failure. Some end in the obscurity of the House of Lords or on the boards of companies, charities or quangos; others end in a blaze of tabloid attention, a moment of national recognition and shame, courtroom drama and perhaps even prison.

It is a terrible thing to admit, but we all love a good political scandal. *Schadenfreude* is indeed shameful – but also delicious. It is made all the more enjoyable if the politician in question is pompous or sanctimonious.

In 1987, US Presidential hopeful Gary Hart challenged the media to 'put a tail on me and see how bored you'll be', which they did and soon uncovered his affair with Donna Rice.

Jonathan Aitken prefaced the campaign to clear his name of lying by staging a press conference at Conservative Central Office, during which he said 'If it falls to me to start a fight to cut out the cancer of bent and twisted journalism in our country with the simple sword of truth and the trusty shield of British fair play, so be it.' Aitken was subsequently sent to prison for perjury and perverting the course of justice. You can imagine the scene as the prison officers relieved him of his possessions on arrival at prison: 'one Rolex watch, one set of keys, chewing gum, one simple sword, one trusty shield ... '

It is getting harder to be brought down by a scandal. In the past, politicians would resign at the first whiff of trouble. Huge Dalton resigned as Chancellor of the Exchequer in 1948 for mentioning in passing some of the detail of one of his budgets to a journalist before delivering it to the House of Commons. Bill Clinton not only survived in office, but was re-elected, against an astonishing backcloth of smears and revelations of sexual misconduct, seduction and rape in the Oval Office (or Oral Office as wags have dubbed it). When you put Clinton's scandals together, it is a wonder he was elected to make the tea, never mind be President. Gennifer Flowers, the draft-dodging, smoking dope but not inhaling, gays in the military, his $200 haircut, the suicide of his associate Vince Foster, the Whitewater affair, Paula Jones, nights in the Lincoln bedroom, and Monica Lewinsky – it all adds up to some good material for Clinton's memoirs.

In Britain, the John Major Government was defined by scandal. It consisted of little else. In a good week, there would be two or three scandals running at the same time. Between September 1992 and December 1996 Ministers David Mellor, Michael Mates, Michael Brown, Tim Smith, Neil Hamilton, Tim Yeo, the Earl of Caithness, Allan Stewart, Robert Hughes, Jonathan Aitken, Rod Richards and David Willetts resigned from the government because of sleaze. Other MPs such as Graham Riddick and David Tredinnick were embroiled in cash-for-questions. Stephen Milligan was found dead after engaging in a dangerous sexual escapade. Others such as John Redwood, Charles Wardle and David Heathcoat-Amory resigned for political reasons, in Redwood's case to try and oust John Major from the top job. The Government, despite attempts at re-launches and policy initiatives, was never more than a fortnight from a scandal for its entire period of office.

Scandal has always been a feature of political life. Francis Bacon was caught accepting bribes; John Wilkes was a womaniser and gambler and was imprisoned for libel; Benjamin Disraeli spent much of his early life being pursued by creditors after losing all his, and others', money in an ill-fated mining investment; Gladstone regularly sought out, and even brought to Downing Street, prostitutes who he claimed he wanted to 'save'; Asquith was a drunkard and Churchill could happily down a bottle of brandy in a single sitting; and Lloyd George was reputed to have had sex with his mistress on the Cabinet Table at Downing Street, and sold peerages for cash. Sex and money have always been attractive to British politicians, and there have always been those willing to risk all – career, status, family – for their allure. 'Power', said Henry Kissinger, 'is a great aphrodisiac'.

Under today's media spotlight, politicians can get away with a lot less than their forebears. Sex maniacs like Lloyd George and John F. Kennedy (who once told Harold Wilson that unless he had a woman at least every three days, he got terrible headaches) carried on without any media attention. Bill Clinton complained that the US media never cut him the same slack that they used to with JFK. The *News of the World* and other tabloids have teams of reporters constantly on the look out for next week's headlines. They follow politicians, talk to their friends and family, even go through their rubbish. The collapse of media deference means that no politician, regardless of status, is safe. Cheque-book journalism ensures that any hotel chambermaid or night porter can sell their titbits of gossip for a tidy profit. The media guarantees that politicians' private lives are public property.

How to deal with a scandal

Some politicians come out of scandals smelling of roses; others up to their necks in manure. How should you handle a scandal if one breaks over you?

The first step is find out who knows what. Who's on to you? Is it the media? Is it your political enemies? Is it a blackmailer? What have they got on you? Are the allegations true? If what is being said is untrue, you should rapidly consult a lawyer and issue a statement to the media. Newspapers will back down unless they are absolutely sure of their ground.

If the answers are that the media have got the story, and its true, you have to make a very swift decision – fight or flight. Do you try to tough it out, or do you resign? If you are going to resign, you should do so immediately, with a statement to the media expressing regret. There is nothing more unseemly than a politician or candidate, mired in sleaze, trying to cling by their fingertips to office. If you're going to go, go in the first few hours of the scandal breaking. That way you may salvage some sympathy and be able to make a come-back. When Peter Mandelson was caught out over a loan he had taken to buy his house, he resigned almost immediately, with his resignation letter sent to the Prime Minister within a day.

Within a few months he was back in government. His close relationship with the Prime Minister helped his position, but his deft handling of the scandal ensured his position could be shored up quickly and that the path back to office was not blocked for ever.

Eighteen months after his return to the Cabinet, however, in a remarkable turn of events, he was caught out again, this time over inappropriate interference in a passport application. The second time round he resigned even faster, not even bothering with a letter but making his statement direct to the television cameras. It seems somewhat likely that he will return for a third go.

If you are not going to go, then you should be prepared for a tough battle. If you decide to stand your ground, you could learn a lot from Paddy Ashdown, the ex-leader of the Liberal Democrats. When confronted by the *News of the World* with evidence of his extra-marital affair, stolen from the safe of his solicitor, Ashdown slapped down an injunction, told his wife, and then held a press conference. By breaking the story himself, and with the support of his wife, he ensured that the scandal did not destroy him, although it did give him the nickname 'Pantsdown'. Ashdown's popularity actually increased in the wake of the affair.

You cannot possibly hope to keep a scandal secret once a newspaper is onto you, so make sure people are getting the information from you before they read about it in their newspapers. Tell your local party officers. Tell your national party press office, so that they can field calls from the media from a position of knowledge. Let your friends and family know, so that they are not shocked or upset by calls from journalists. Shore up your position, and get your allies to issue statements of support.

Recent scandals have been characterised by strategic deployment of the ultimate weapon – the loyal wife. When Bill and Hillary appeared on television during the Gennifer Flowers scandal they presented a united front. When David Mellor was embroiled in the Antonia de Sancha affair, with made-up tales of Chelsea football strips and toe-sucking, he appeared at the garden gate with his wife loyally by his side (shortly before getting divorced). Jeffrey Archer always has the fragrant Mary at his side in times of trouble. The appearance of the loyal wife gives the message to the public – if my wife can forgive me, so should you.

You need a good lawyer on standby. Some of the wilder rumours about senior politicians doing the rounds have been kept out of newspapers by threats of legal action. If you have been libelled, be prepared to fight your corner, either through the Press Complaints Commission, or in the Courts.

The moments after the scandal breaking are the moments when your future will be decided. Like the moments when the Emperor's thumb hovers over the fate of a gladiator, your future will be decided in minutes not hours.

Top tips for dealing with a scandal
1 Find out who knows what as fast as possible
2 Decide whether its 'fight or flight'
3 Tell your loved ones and your party bosses
4 Shore up your supporters and secure their support
5 Get your rebuttal in fast
6 Don't try to laugh it off
7 Don't take the moral high ground – it's just further to fall
8 Resign in a way that means you can come back.

Gaffes

Because politicians never stop talking, the law of averages dictates that from time to time they will say something which their ever-vigilant opponents can declare a 'gaffe'. A gaffe is when a politician says something they shouldn't. Often it may be a perfectly innocuous remark, or even the truth, but your opponents will leap on it as though it was an admission of drug dealing. Gaffes can be an off-the-cuff remark or humorous remark which can be twisted or backfires on you. Some gaffes haunt the perpetrator for years to come.

John F. Kennedy announced to confused Germans that he was a doughnut when he said 'Ich bin ein Berliner' . You can bet that Norman Lamont wishes he'd never said 'Je ne regrette rien' when asked if he regretted Britain's humiliating devaluation in 1992, or that he sang in his bath, or that he saw 'green shoots of recovery' in the depths of the recession. Edwina Currie caused chaos when she claimed that most eggs had salmonella, and caused offence when she asserted that 'people in the north die of ignorance and crisps.' Brian Mawhinney gaffed when he blamed loony left Camden for supporting the 'Hopscotch Asian Women's Group' which turned out to be Home Office funded with the Princess Royal as its patron. Alan Clark couldn't understand the fuss over his reference to 'Bongo Bongo' land in 1985.

Sometimes modern technology can catch people out. When Richard Needham said over his mobile phone 'I wish that cow would resign' referring to Margaret Thatcher, he was recorded and broadcast. When John Major called three of his Cabinet colleagues 'bastards' he did not realise nearby microphones were recording his true opinions.

The closest Tony Blair came to a gaffe during the 1997 campaign was when he referred to the proposed Scottish Parliament as having tax raising powers 'like any parish council'. This was twisted to mean that he thought the Parliament would be unimportant.

If you gaffe, the only thing to do is apologise as quickly and loudly as possible. An apology will hopefully end the matter. If you try to tough it out, or explain what you meant, your opponents will hound you and keep the matter running longer than it should.

Dirty tricks

When politicians become desperate, or when their campaigns go out of control, they resort to dirty tricks. Dirty tricks are difficult to define, because the definition depends on where you are standing. When, in the last week of the US Presidential election in 2000, it came to light that George W. Bush had a prosecution for drink-driving about which he had not been totally forthcoming, was it an example of dirty tricks? The information had been dug out by supporters of the Democrats, and it's timing, just days before Polling Day, was designed to inflict maximum damage to the Bush campaign. But didn't the American electorate have a right to know that the man they might vote in as President was arrested for drink driving, and then hoped no-one would find out? In a contest like the Bush-Gore election where the margins between the candidates was wafer-thin, such a revelation could have had a devastating effect.

The most famous example of dirty tricks in politics is Watergate, which has given headline writers the opportunity to suffix every subsequent exposé of political dirty tricks or scandal with '–gate'. Watergate is the name of the hotel in Washington, USA, where covert operatives (codenamed 'the Plumbers'), acting on the instructions of the President of the United States, Richard Nixon, were caught red-handed breaking into the party offices of his political rivals the Democrats to try to steal secrets. The scandal revealed a culture of paranoia and disregard for the law at the heart of the Nixon administration, which culminated in his impeachment as President.

In Britain, one general election was largely decided by the use of dirty tricks. In 1924, the short-lived first Labour Government was voted out of office after a news story broke about a letter from the President of the Communist International, Zinoviev. The letter, sent to the British Communists, called for increased Communist activity and 'the revolutionising of the international and British proletariat' if Labour won the election. One Labour Minister, on reading the headlines, said 'we're sunk', and he was right – Labour lost the election. It was the first, but not the last, use of the 'reds-under-the-beds' scare tactic. In 1998, 74 years after the Zinoviev letter was leaked to the press, it was revealed as a forgery, written by the Security Services and leaked to sympathetic right-wing journalists.

Dirty tricks may be a feature of modern politics, notably in the United States, but if campaigns can be fought, no matter how fiercely, on issues and arguments rather than personal attacks and the 'character question', then democracy will be better for it. The evidence is that revelations of politicians' sleaze, sex, and suspect behaviour does not merely damage individual politicians, it damages politics. The dirt that gets thrown around ends up soiling the whole political process, and the voters switch off and stay at home.

8   'I Therefore Declare ...'

At the culmination of the campaign comes the count, where the votes are counted, the results announced, and the candidates elected. This is the final act in the election drama, and like the rest of the campaign, has its own ritual and conventions. The candidate may feel exhausted and as though there is nothing else to be done, but the job is not over yet. At the count, the candidate is still on duty, and still has functions to perform.

In every parliamentary constituency, the count is conducted separately by local authority staff, under the watchful eye of the Returning Officer. For local elections, all the seats are counted simultaneously, with results being announced in quick succession. Counts are usually conducted in a large central location like a community centre or town hall, and are ticket-only affairs. Candidates and their friends and family are allocated tickets, as are agents, campaign teams and the media.

After the end of the polls, there is a gap of a few hours while all the ballot boxes are collected and the counting starts. In rural areas it can take hours to collect all the ballot boxes from outlying polling stations. As the candidate, you should use this precious few hours to get some sleep, have a shower and change your clothes, because election counts can go on for hours, into the early hours of the morning and they are highly charged affairs.

At the count itself, there is a lot of nervous energy, chatter between campaigners and journalists, and waiting in a state of anticipation. In a general election, the media focuses on certain seats which are of special interest - either because they are key seats which help determine the outcome of the election, or because they are the seats of the main political party leaders. The television cameras were at Huntingdon and Sedgefield in force at the 1997 general election, not because those seats were likely to change hands, but because they were the seats of John Major and Tony Blair.

Each candidate appoints 'counting agents' from his or her campaign team to watch the conduct of the count and to ensure that votes are properly counted and allocated to the right candidate. They are usually counted into bundles of fifty, and fifty votes on the wrong pile can make the difference between victory and defeat, so the role of the counting agents is not to be taken lightly. Events in Florida in 2000 prove the point. You can see the piles get higher for each candidate and a trained eye can discern who is ahead as the count proceeds.

If, after recounts, the vote is tied and there is no winner, the election is settled by drawing lots, or even tossing a coin.

Eventually, the result is in, and the Returning Officer will inform the candidates and their agents privately before announcing the result. The result is not official until it is formally 'declared' by the Returning Officer with the time-honoured phrase 'I therefore declare the winner ... ', but is known to the candidates, campaign teams and media a few minutes in advance. This gives you a short time to perfect your 'Gosh I've won' or stoical-in-defeat look.

If the result is very close, you and your agent have the right to 'call for a recount'. Recounts mean that the whole process is repeated, and sometimes the result of the election changes as a result. Recounts can be conducted as many times as you like, as long as there is a candidate who rejects the outcome and calls for one. In the USA, the 2000 Presidential election result was delayed for weeks because of endless recounts by hand in Florida. The archaic system of marking ballot-papers with a hole-punching device meant that many voters expressed a clear preference by creating an indentation, or chad, without punching a hole in the ballot paper, and thus a whole new lexicon of chads, pregnant chads, and hanging chads entered the language.

In the end, though, even for Al Gore and George W. Bush, there is only victory or defeat. There is no prize for coming second in politics. There will be one of two outcomes to all the months of campaigning and years of preparation: you will either win or lose. Either way, you should be prepared to deal with each eventuality.

How to win

You've won. You may feel like punching the air with joy, sticking two fingers up at your rivals and drinking champagne from the bottle, but such exuberance must be avoided, at least until you are safely away from the public and media gaze. Candidates who have won are expected to behave with decorum and magnanimity. You have not won *Who Wants to be a Millionaire*, you have been given a serious job to do. The manner with which you conduct yourself at the moment of triumph is the very first test.

Stay calm. Allow yourself a smile, and a cheery wave to your supporters. You can be excused a 'Blimey!' look of surprise, *à la* Stephen Twigg in Enfield Southgate in 1997. But triumphalism must be avoided. You must shake the hands of the people you have defeated and thank them for fighting a good fight.

In your victory speech you must pay tribute to the candidates you have beaten. You must thank the police and the returning officer and their staff. You must thank your volunteers. Most of all you must thank the people who have just elected you, and make a public pledge to serve them diligently and dutifully. If you have just unseated a sitting politician, you must have something positive to say about them, regardless of what you have just spent your campaign saying about them.

Take the leaf from Tony Blair's speech to his new MPs in the wake of Labour's 1997 landslide, when he said 'we are not the masters now; the people are the masters. We are the servants of the people.' Such dutiful sentiment can go down very well with those who have just elected you.

How to lose

You've lost. You want to cry, shout, get drunk, go home and sleep for a week. Whatever emotions of disappointment overtake you, you must stay in control. You should view an election defeat as a temporary setback, not the end of all your ambitions. You may have lost the battle, but not the war. On the night of 1 May 1997, many astonishing general election results took place all over the country, but two of them, only a few miles apart, illustrate perfectly how a candidate can lose with honour and how to be a bad loser. The first was Enfield Southgate, where darling of the right, Michael Portillo, lost to Labour's Stephen Twigg, and the other was Putney, where the scandal-ridden former Minister, David Mellor, lost to Labour's Tony Coleman.

Michael Portillo's defeat was a shock result for all concerned, but

Portillo's dignified behaviour on the night earned him plaudits, even from his enemies, and ensured that he could find his way back into Parliament just a few years later. He was reserved and stoical, and heaped praise on the opponent who had just ousted him. He stayed calm and measured. He even showed some remorse. His handling of his defeat marked the start of his recovery.

David Mellor, by contrast, used his defeat speech to attack James Goldsmith and the Referendum Party for 'attempting to buy the British political system', and to tell him to 'get back to your hacienda'. This caused uproar on the platform, which consisted of a number of joke candidates including a huge transsexual with flashing breasts. Mellor's career came to a sad, chaotic and undignified end.

So if you've lost, remember that politics is a marathon not a sprint and that comebacks are always possible. Lose with dignity. Go with honour and your head held high. And then start to plan your comeback. Revenge, after all, is a dish best served cold.

Top tips for election night

1 Get some sleep before the count
2 Appoint eagle-eyed counting agents – every vote counts
3 Stay sober
4 Remain calm and collected – after all, it's only politics
5 Have a short speech prepared for both eventualities
6 Lose with dignity or win with magnanimity
7 Thank those who have helped you – the people you meet on the way up are the same ones you meet on the way down.

Conclusion

Campaigning in a Post-Modern World

So there you have it – how to win an election. All you need is a rational, informed electorate, perfect political intelligence and polling, trustworthy, exciting politicians, a balanced and intelligent political media, brilliant communications, and a well-organised and well-resourced local campaign machine staffed by trained enthusiastic volunteers.

The realities of campaigning fall far short from this campaigners' idyll. Campaigns are random, ramshackle affairs, held together with string and sellotape. Political campaigning, like politics itself, is dynamic, fluid, and ever-changing. There are trends which can be discerned and trajectories which can be identified. The influence of American election techniques can be overstated, but clearly exists on British campaigns, especially as long as New Labour's love affair with the US political gurus persists. So if we want to know where campaigning will go in the next few years, we might look across the Atlantic for clues.

But British political campaigns will retain and develop their own characteristics, driven by our own political structures, cultures, and national identity. In some ways, we may be ahead of the game in the development of campaign techniques. We may be spared the excesses of US politics by our stricter laws on spending on campaigns, and the British distaste for negative campaigning or personal attacks. Our sense of fair play may yet save us from the depths of gutter-politics.

Campaigns will continue to professionalise, as any lingering hostility to the slick skills of the communications industries is dispelled by real election victories in real elections. We will, within a few years, see campaign consultants – political mercenaries for hire – emerge from the ranks of the

UK-based public affairs and public relations companies as a distinct new form of consultant.

As John Arnold of UK-based consultancy Politicsdirect.com says 'the next few years will see specialist campaign communications experts setting up in Britain, offering campaign skills and techniques to parties and candidates. What is the norm in the USA will become the norm here in Britain.'

The worlds of political campaigning and advertising, marketing and PR will become increasingly blurred, as political parties contract out their campaigning activities and buy in expertise on a campaign-by-campaign basis. Political communications and advertising, revolutionised by first Margaret Thatcher and then Peter Mandelson, will seek out new ways of communicating politics to an increasingly sceptical electorate.

A group of academics concluded after the 1997 general election that 'the rise of post-modern campaigns, characterised by a more autonomous and fragmented media, more professionalised strategic communications by parties and a more dealigned electorate, creates new challenges for effective communications and voters in a mediated democracy.'

The new challenges which the academics refer to, stemming from this fragmented media and dealigned electorate, might include:

- Adaptation of direct marketing techniques to political campaigning, particularly direct mail and 'relationship marketing', based on a long-term, on-going, informed dialogue between parties and voters *as individuals* rather than classes, or social groups. The days of 'safe seats' 'heartlands' and 'core voters' will soon be the stuff of history. Every vote will be fought for, and none taken for granted.

- Maximising the opportunities of the information revolution, especially the Internet, to reach voters, consult voters, raise awareness and funds, and provoke political action, without excluding the 'information poor' from democracy. The Internet represents the greatest opportunities for political campaigners to connect with the people.

- Engaging voters via political campaigns in new forms of democratic involvement, beyond the traditional 'vote for us, we know best' approach.

Living in a democracy will mean much more than strolling down to the school hall once every five years to stuff a ballot paper into a tin box.

If politicians and their advisers can meet these challenges, explore new forms of engagement and dialogue, communicate without patronising or trivialising, and reinvigorate our politics, then democracy, in new and unforeseen forms, may stand a chance of survival in a world of corporate giants and bureaucratic monoliths. The people may retain a say over their lives.

But whatever the tough challenges ahead, and the social and economic forces which drive political change, it is clear that the political campaign will remain at the heart of political activity. For as long as politicians want to win votes, campaigns will exist to persuade voters to give their support. Elements of campaigns in the future will be the same as the ones familiar to us. There will still be the rain-soaked but undaunted activist with a shopping carrier full of newsletters and leaflets, the candidate kissing babies, the glitzy rally, the wary voter answering the knock on the door. In this, political campaigning in the next decades would be familiar to Harold Wilson, Winston Churchill or William Gladstone. In other ways – vote-catching in cyberspace, the online hustings, the personalised e-election address – campaigning will seem strange and unfamiliar. Changes will creep up on us. As recently as 1992, senior Labour politicians were issued with phonecards for public phone boxes in order to keep communications open during the campaign. One told me that her top tips for what to take campaigning were 'lots of pairs of tights and a stack of ten pence pieces for the phone.'

Now, every candidate is electronically tagged to their party managers with pager, mobile and email, although clean tights remain a must. The communications revolution is engulfing all areas of our lives with only passing notice from most of us, including campaign communications.

Political campaigns will continue to battle with apathy and cynicism, and still intrude on the householder trying to watch *Coronation Street* who says they are 'not political and never vote.' But campaigns will remain at the heart of democracy, and exist to get people elected. In this sense, campaigns are the start of the journey, not the end. They may lead to defeat, but far more frightening for the candidate should be the prospect that they lead to your election. That's when the fun really starts, as this poem by Roger McGough shows:

The Leader

I wanna be the leader
I wanna be the leader
Can I be the leader?
Can I? I can?
Promise? Promise?
Yippee, I'm the leader
I'm the leader
OK what shall we do?

Select Bibliography

Anonymous   *Primary Colors* (Chatto and Windus, 1996)
Bike, William   *Winning Political Campaigns* (Denali Press, 1998)
BMP DDB   *How the Left Learned to Love Advertising* (2000)
Hobday, Peter   *Managing the Message* (London House, 2000)
Gould, Philip   *The Unfinished Revolution – How the modernisers saved the Labour Party* (Little Brown, 1998)
Kavanagh, Dennis   *Election Campaigning – The New Marketing of Politics* (Blackwell, 1995)
Morris, Dick   *Vote.com* (Renaissance, 1999)
Morris, Dick   *The New Prince* (Renaissance, 1999)
Norris, Pippa et al   *On Message – communicating the campaign* (Sage, 1999)
O'Farrell, John   *Things Can Only Get Better* (Doubleday, 1998)
Richards, Paul   *Be Your Own Spin Doctor* (Take That, 1998)
Rosenbaum, Martin   *From Soapbox to Soundbite* (Macmillan, 1997)
Scammell, Margaret   *Designer Politics – how elections are won* (Macmillan, 1995)

Index

A

Abse, Leo 90
Activists 26, 27
Adam Smith Institute 35
Additional Member System 9
Adonis, Andrew 15
Advertising xv, 143, 144
Agents 25, 55
Aitken, Jonathan 162
Akehurst, Luke 86
Anecdotes 95
Any Questions 127
Apathy 15
Appearance 74, 128
Archer, Jeffrey 165
Aristotle 25
Arnold, John 174
Ashdown, Paddy 164
Asquith, H. H. 163
Attlee, Clement 101

B

Background research 63
Bacon, Francis 163
Bailey, Adrian 11
Baker, Norman xviii
Baldwin, Stanley 41
Barnard, Alan 42
Beards 75

Behavioural scientists xv
Bell, Martin x, xvi, 38
Beloff, Nora xiv
Benjy the Bin Man 24
Benn, Hilary 39
Benn, Tony xix, 7, 15, 97, 129, 153
Bercow, John x
Bevan, Aneurin 88, 92
Bevin, Ernest xvi
Biden, Joe 96
Billericay xviii
Blair, Tony ix, x, xiv, 4, 12, 44, 63,
   64, 66, 74, 89, 91, 96, 104,
   106, 107, 132, 133, 134, 153,
   166
Blitzing 83
Blunkett, David 39
Boothroyd, Betty x, 6
Braggins, John 7, 42
Brooke, Peter 4
Brown, George 93
Brown, Gordon 33, 45, 92, 98
Brown, Michael 162
Bush, George Snr 107
Bush, George W. xv, 97, 166
Bushfire polls 65
Butler, David 18
By-elections 6, 7